A God at the Door

Also by Tishani Doshi

Poetry

Girls Are Coming Out of the Woods
Everything Begins Elsewhere
Countries of the Body

Fiction

Small Days and Nights
Fountainville
The Pleasure Seekers

Other

The Adulterous Citizen: Poems, Stories, Essays
Madras Then, Chennai Now (with Pramod Kapoor and Nanditha Krishna)

A God at the Door

Tishani Doshi

COPPER CANYON PRESS
PORT TOWNSEND, WASHINGTON

Cover art: Olivia Fraser, *Darshan III*, 2019, 11 x 22 in. Pigment, Arabic gum and gold leaf on handmade Sanganer paper.

Copper Canyon Press is in residence at Fort Worden State Park in Port Townsend, Washington, under the auspices of Centrum. Centrum is a gathering place for artists and creative thinkers from around the world, students of all ages and backgrounds, and audiences seeking extraordinary cultural enrichment.

Library of Congress Cataloging-in-Publication Data
Names: Doshi, Tishani, 1975- author.
Title: A god at the door / Tishani Doshi.
Description: Port Towznsend, Washington : Copper Canyon Press, [2022] |
    Summary: "In an era of pandemic lockdown and brutal politics, Tishani Doshi's
    poems make vital space for what must come next-the return of wonder and free
    movement, and a profound sense of connection to what matters most. From
    a microscopic cell to flightless birds, to a sumo wrestler and the tree of life,
    Doshi interrupts the news cycle to pause in grief or delight, to restore power to
    language. A God at the Door invites the reader on a pilgrimage—one that leads
    us back to the sacred temple of ourselves. This is an exquisite, generous collection
    from a poet at the peak of her powers"— Provided by publisher.
Identifiers: LCCN 2021025504 | ISBN 9781556594526 (paperback)
Subjects: LCGFT: Poetry.
Classification: LCC PR9499.4.D67 G63 2021 | DDC 821/.92—dc23
LC record available at https://lccn.loc.gov/2021025504

98765432 first printing

Copper Canyon Press
Post Office Box 271
Port Townsend, Washington 98368
www.coppercanyonpress.org

Acknowledgments

Grateful acknowledgment is made to the following journals, in which some of these poems first appeared:

Brooklyn Rail: "Macroeconomics," "Mandala," "Survival"

Dhaka Tribune: "Contagion," "Together"

Granta: "Cell," "Collective," "Cosmos," "Nation," "Self," "Species"

The Hindu: "What Mr. Frog Running Away from Marilyn Monroe Taught Me about #MeToo"

Indian Express: "The Coronapocalypse Will Be Televised"

The Indian Quarterly: "Creation Abecedarian," "Microeconomics," "A Possible Explanation as to Why We Mutilate Women & Trees, Which Tries to End on a Note of Hope"

Literary Hub: "Listening to Abida Parveen on Loop, I Understand Why I Miss Home and Why It Must Be So"

Magma: "Do Not Go Out in the Storm," "Hope Is the Thing"

The Moth: "My Loneliness Is Not the Same as Your Loneliness," "Poems Lull Us into Safety"

Narrative: "The Stormtroopers of My Country"

New Humanist: "Everyone Has a Wilting Point"

The New York Review of Books: "Advice for Pliny the Elder, Big Daddy of Mansplainers"

Open: "End-of-Year Epiphany at the Holiday Inn," "Every Unbearable Thing"

Pangyrus: "Instructions on Surviving Genocide"

Plume: "Pilgrimage"

Poetry: "They Killed Cows. I Killed Them."

Poetry Wales: "In a Dream I Give Birth to a Sumo Wrestler," "Variations on Hippo"

The Punch Magazine: "Postcard to My Mother-in-Law Who at Sixteen Is Chasing Brigitte Bardot in Saint-Tropez"

Rattle: "After a Shooting in a Maternity Clinic in Kabul," "Tree of Life"

Tin House: "I Found a Village and in It Were All Our Missing Women"

Virginia Quarterly Review: "We Will Not Kill You. We'll Just Shoot You in the Vagina."

Wasafiri: "It Has Taken Many Years to See My Body"

"A Dress Is Like a Field" was commissioned by *Vogue* India for the anthology *Dress,* 2018.

"Homage to the Square" was commissioned by Studio Wayne McGregor, 2018.

"Many Good and Wonderful Things" was commissioned by the Hay Festival to commemorate the centenary of Armistice Day, 2018.

"Roots" was commissioned by the Bradford Literature Festival to commemorate Frida Kahlo, 2019.

"Tiger Woman" was commissioned by the *Royal Academy of Arts Magazine,* 2020.

"A Blue Mormon Finds Herself among Common Emigrants" was anthologized in *Tales of Two Planets,* Penguin Books, 2020 (edited by John Freeman).

"Face Exercises for Marionette Lines" was anthologized in *Spark,* Blue Diode Publishing, 2018 (edited by Rob A. Mackenzie and Louise Peterkin).

"Petard" was anthologized in *No News,* Recent Work Press, 2020 (edited by Paul Munden, Alvin Pang, and Shane Strange).

"Why the Brazilian Butt Lift Won't Save Us" was anthologized in *A Thousand Cranes for India,* Seagull Books, 2020 (edited by Pallavi Aiyar).

Thanks as well to Varuna, the Writers' House and Civitella Ranieri, where some of these poems were written, and to Carlo Pizzati and Deborah Kapchan, who read early drafts of these poems.

The book's epigraphs are taken from *I Lalla: the Poems of Lal Děd,* translated from the Kashmiri by Ranjit Hoskote (Penguin Classics, 2011) and Lorrie Moore's short story "Joy" from *The Collected Stories* (Faber & Faber, 2009).

For my father, Vinod, whose name means joy.

I trapped my breath in the bellows of my throat:
a lamp blazed up inside, showed me who I really was.
I crossed the darkness holding fast to that lamp,
scattering its light-seeds around me as I went.

LAL DĚD

The world was lovely, really, but it was tricky,
and peevish with the small things, like a god
who didn't get out much.

LORRIE MOORE

Contents

Mandala • 3

Pilgrimage • 4

Creation Abecedarian • 5

The Stormtroopers of My Country • 6

My Loneliness Is Not the Same as Your Loneliness • 7

A Blue Mormon Finds Herself among Common Emigrants • 10

Why the Brazilian Butt Lift Won't Save Us • 12

Every Unbearable Thing • 14

Advice for Pliny the Elder, Big Daddy of Mansplainers • 17

Roots • 18

In a Dream I Give Birth to a Sumo Wrestler • 20

Instructions on Surviving Genocide • 22

The Comeback of Speedos • 27

Face Exercises for Marionette Lines • 28

I Found a Village and in It Were All Our Missing Women • 30

Contagion • 32

Tree of Life • 33

Homage to the Square • 35

I Don't Want to Be Remembered for My Last Instagram Post • 37

Everyone Has a Wilting Point • 39

Tigress Hugs Manchurian Fir • 41

Poems Lull Us into Safety • 42

After a Shooting in a Maternity Clinic in Kabul • 43

They Killed Cows. I Killed Them. • 45

Cell • 49

Self • 50

Collective • 51

Nation • 52

Species • 53

Cosmos • 54

The Coronapocalypse Will Be Televised • 57

Variations on Hippo • 59

A Dress Is Like a Field • 63

Postcard to My Mother-in-Law Who at
Sixteen Is Chasing Brigitte Bardot in Saint-Tropez • 65

Together • 66

Many Good and Wonderful Things • 67

I Carry My Uterus in a Small Suitcase • 69

Bacterium • 70

A Possible Explanation as to Why We Mutilate
Women & Trees, Which Tries to End on a Note of Hope • 71

What Mr. Frog Running Away from Marilyn Monroe
Taught Me about #MeToo • 73

Tiger Woman • 75

We Will Not Kill You. We'll Just Shoot You in the Vagina. • 76

Microeconomics • 81

Macroeconomics • 83

This May Reach You Either as a Bird or Flower • 84

Petard • 85

Rotten Grief • 86

October Fugue • 88

Do Not Go Out in the Storm • 89

Listening to Abida Parveen on Loop, I Understand
Why I Miss Home and Why It Must Be So • 92

End-of-Year Epiphany at the Holiday Inn • 94

It Has Taken Many Years to See My Body • 96

Hope Is the Thing • 99

Survival • 101

Notes • 103

About the Author • 109

A God at the Door

MANDALA

Anyone who believes a leaf is just a leaf is missing
the point. In the attic, there's a picture of gingko
growing steadily yellow, while the body
of gingko remains evergreen. He works his way
through opium dens and bordellos. I'd like to tell you
not to worry. Reality has a way of sorting itself out,
but panic is infectious. The scare arrives when you're doing
jumping jacks or organizing the cutlery, some moment of low
cosmological drama. Interrupted by the discovery of a lump.
Or the nine o'clock news. Suddenly, every door handle is a death
sentence. How lonely it must have been for the first astronomers,
freezing on their terraces, trying to catch the light of faraway moons.
Sometimes it's hard to know whether you're slowing down
or speeding up. Time's wobbly trampoline confuses us.
We stitch our days and nights, one to the other,
and it's like embroidering a galaxy, but even galaxies
recede from one another. Once, a woman played my body
as though it were a harp. I slept on a wooden plank
and she strummed the strings below until I became
a whale shark, pounding through the oceans. I emerged
as if out of a wormhole, more or less intact. For days I felt fins
where my cheeks should have been. We talk of bodies
as though we could not understand the universe within them,
even though we've all gaped at the stump of a tree
and understood that time moves outward in a circle.
And while everything seems endless, there's always a ring
of something permeable holding us in. Sometimes we leave
the house without our masks and it's a relief to take a break
from who we are. Dwarf star, prayer bell, lone stag
feeding in the gorse—something will hold a mirror
to our faces, when all we need is to be led upstairs.

PILGRIMAGE

Every now and then the universe hands out treats.
A cryogenic pod for Christmas, a family trip
to Greece. We stare like pigeons at our feeders,
impatient for the next gift to drop, sprouting stress bars
on our feathers at the bounty of some other pigeon's trough.
We were taught to show devotion by walking in circles.
We had visions in caves and when the host served an aperitif
of fermented mare's milk, we drank it with grace.
We walked barefoot, keeping the center to our right,
measured paces between shrines in twilight. These days
we take the video coach, but still bring baskets of marigold.
In times of war we go from cot to cot, whispering sweet nothings
into soldiers' ears. We write letters to their beloveds and preserve
their relics—toothpick, comb, bone. How else to arrive
at the ecstasy of ourselves if we cannot see another's body?
The world has its unknown territories, its dragons.
We wander about with blindfolds, shouting *Marco.*
Only the devil responds *Polo.* It is all remembrance. To repeat
and repeat again the names of what we deem holy.
Sometimes we move so far we forget where we've been.
It's like looking at an old picture of your face. The earth holds
all our dead, all our half-eaten apples, and still it has space.
We make circuits around history with lamps
and portable altars of fire, feel the thrill of ghosting in the footsteps
of gods and demons. Remember this hill where you were crucified,
this spot in the river where you tore out your breast and flung it
at the cursed city. Remember this sky you forgot in your room,
confusing the blue of the screen for the cosmos within.
No matter how many nights you spend in exile,
remember, pilgrim, you come home to this skin.

CREATION ABECEDARIAN

As each day passes we grow less certain about the universe.
Bewildered by black holes and big bangs, our textbooks confuse
childbirth with cosmic eggs, skim over the functions of reproduction.
Darwin was wrong, they claim, not just about his theory of biological
evolution, but about everything. We are descendants of sages!
From Primordial Man's mouth, arms, thighs, feet we sprang.
God is an organizational genius. Even our Minister of Education,
holistic scholar and yogi, believes our forefathers never stated
in writing or on their dictaphones that they ever saw an ape
jolted into being a man. It never happened.
Know, of course, our people were daubing their wrists with
lotus perfume while elsewhere others were chiseling rocks. Still,
Mary's immaculate hijab notwithstanding, most women I know
need to get on all fours to accept beans into their navels,
or lay eggs in a petri dish to set the marigolds abloom in spring.
Perhaps we're like the pyramids of Giza and must remain enigmatic
quandaries. Never mind DNA. Yesterday, I was stalked by a cheeky
rhesus macaque through gardens of tamarind in the Theosophical
Society. Whenever I stopped to look back at him, he'd stop
too and turn quizzically. When I ran, he ran faster,
until I couldn't tell who was who anymore, the gap between us closed.
Valmiki and Virgil, sages both, wrote of transformations in the forest.
We're all pushing for reinvention like caterpillars chewing through
xenia, unaware of the rudimentary wings tucked into our bodies.
You and I may never be butterflies, but we recognize each other,
zoomorphic ancestor. We bow and reach for that invisible thing that beats.

THE STORMTROOPERS OF MY COUNTRY

The stormtroopers of my country love
their wives but are okay to burn
what needs to be burned for the good
of the republic often doing so in brown
pleated shorts and cute black hats with sticks

and tear gas and manifestos of love
for cows for heritage for hard Hindu burning
devotion for motherland tongue it's all good
their pants are buckled unbuckled brown
shut up this is serious this country will stick

it to infiltrators imprison traitors love
neighbors with the right papers you know burn
baby imagine a country a house on fire good
gen z millennial kids good upstarts brown
denizens who've discovered their rights are sticks

are legs to walk the streets dearly beloved
we are gathered here as effigies to burn
standing up so take your anticitizen laws good
sir good government ha-ha off-color joke brown
out shit I wish we had the internet because sticks

may break us but this is a revolution of love
like the sixties gauchistes hate me but don't burn
public property really sir you promised us good
governance but the evidence is mounting of brown
soldiers massacring brown shops mosques stick

with the pogrom atrocity death march love
march no such thing as a clean termite to burn
is to purify oh our culture so ancient so good
we're in the thick of the swastika now no brow
beating will divide us together we must stick

My Loneliness Is Not the Same as Your Loneliness

My loneliness is not the same
as your loneliness, although they send
each other postcards and when they meet
they relax enough to nap
on each other's sofas.

> I've never felt more alone
> than when I was being burgled,
> our bodies facing one another,
> the burglar and me. Can I help,
> I asked but really what I was saying
> was, Stay, don't leave.

You say you're sometimes jolted awake
by the horror of eating animals,
how most mornings it passes,
but once, you walked downstairs to find
a watermelon had exploded on your table,
all that rotten red froth seeping
through the tablecloth

> and even though I understood
> this explosion exploded something
> in you, that it has to do with bodies—
> animal, watermelon, burglar, your body
> and mine, the thread between us,
> I could not reach for your hand,
> could not say, Don't live among strangers.

They say it starts in childhood,
or being alive in a large country where
all the roads are empty and lead in.
They say go east, go west, go somewhere,
start something, but where can you go
if you don't know how to manage thirsty

buffaloes, if the past is a birdcage
that grows larger the farther away
from home you get?

I left town, hit a patch of feeling blue,
called you. Funny story, you said,
Puppy just shredded eighteen volumes
of the *Mahabharata*.
What's happening
with you?

I say, You know, I'm on the road,
it's the underground guerilla life for me,
dirt and celibacy. All I can hear
are birds and sirens, and sometimes,
birds imitating sirens.

We're quick to tell each other
It's okay, it's okay, we can't all
be preceded or followed by something.
We can't all carry around tanks of oxygen
or storm through doors reeking
of whiskey and Pernod.

There's no known cure.
It isn't true about daily B_{12} shots
or living in a commune. In wars
there are almost always the same number
dead from starving as from combat.
Whatever it is, it lives in the body
and will stay till the body
runs aground.

Singers say they hear the next note
before they sing it. My loneliness
is something like that. I know
not just what it is, but how
it will sound.

There's a child screaming
in the playground below, a refrain
so shrill it scrapes a layer off the air.
She's reassuring herself, she's not alone.
No one tells her, We're here together,
you've been heard.

A Blue Mormon Finds Herself among Common Emigrants

after Cavafy

It's uncertain why they're here.

Pretty sure it's the same old sob story—
    no food in the fields, government gassing their kids,
        neighbors throwing bombs on their homes.

Shall we go down to the shore and save them?

They have such short lives,
    such unpronounceable names.

Wouldn't it be better if they stayed put?

Do they watch clouds or collect shells? Can we know?

So many die along the way.

Think about their lives in far Bombay—
    subsisting on the undersides of leaves,
        trying not to get shot in the head
            while hanging upside down from a tree.

Think of Nabokov, that crafty taxonomist,
    filling notecards with their habits—
        "The Original Climate Refugees."

I spoke to one—a Blue Mormon.

Do you know how difficult it is to be so beautiful? she said.

Stuff happens to beautiful creatures. It's unsettling.

All those nets and hours in glass jars,
    all those snot-nosed boys playing pin the specimen.

Did I mention they have a fanatical approach to breeding?

Sometimes, the Blue Mormon complained,
    when we don't get enough food, we emerge as dwarves.

This is distressing.

How to explain there are no perfect conditions?
          There's always too little rain or too much.
                    Someone's bound to give you a bad TripAdvisor review.

All this swarming across highways in lemon ribbons
          of heat, clustering around hilltops and lakes, when
                    they could gather less visibly in locations less elite.

Goes without saying they'll seduce our old parents
                    and get them to sign away the property deeds.
                              Our wives will soon be kneeling at altars of ixora.

We must proceed with caution.

Maybe we could give them wristbands or pin
                    yellow stars to their tails. Maybe we should build fences
                              or draw crosses on the winglike doors of their tents.

In America at least, they fix them with sensors
                              to monitor where they go.

We must think about the environment.

It's too soon to talk of deportation.

Certainly, it would be barbaric to separate
                              children from their parents.

How shameful the aberrant Blue Mormon is,

shrugging off her feathery vest,
          singing her sad song of asylum.

Do you think I'd be fleeing if I didn't have to?
          They're just insects. But me—I'm different, can't you see?

Why the Brazilian Butt Lift Won't Save Us

The body refuses happiness.
That was once upon a time,
that was long ago when you could run naked
through a field without consternation.
You and your perfectly sized baby parts.

The body grows dissatisfied
once it starts towering over dogs
and staring into the hearts of kitchen counters.

Pretty soon your alter-body
is calling from a downtown phone booth
saying, *Listen, baby, you need to step up the retinoids.*

We know, don't we, that a forest is being
truncheoned as we speak. That a girl in that forest
is being truncheoned too. A girl, or a hundred.
That all the words we have for *my heart can't take
it anymore* won't be able to describe
what happens to the body at the end of that.

Still, the body wants to be glorious while it can.

It sees lips burgeoning like a Hokusai wave
and thinks, I'll have some of that. It sees bones Caravaggio
might have dreamed of and microbladed eyebrows
and neat marble apples the size of a generously cupped hand,
and says, *Yes, yes, yes.* But mostly, it sees
Kim Kardashian's ass rising like a mountain
out of the Atlantic, and thinks, I, too,
want to oversee a metropolis.

And why shouldn't it?

Aren't we all trying to get back to a time
before the blemishes? When the body
was carefree with no stretch marks
and pristine platelet-rich hair—

an origami crane built to withstand
the damaging effects of light,
gusting on thermals to fly
against any mushroom cloud.

So what's a few small wounds to the forehead?

What's a needle the size of your life?

Every Unbearable Thing

say you began as rib or clod
of earth say you were blossoming
until someone stared too long
at your shirt and leaned in
unbuttoned pushed forced
don't mistake me   this is not
a poem against longing
but against the kind of one-way
desire that herds you into
a dead-end alley and how this can
lead to a weakened epidermis
and despair and nights of howling
and whom can you tell except
mother   friend   cat
while sky keeps on being sky
and streets fill with danger

say you survive and mostly
you're okay because turns
out you can carry cauldrons
of hurt and your heart is
as strong as a giant carbon atom
say you gather sisters and tell
one another legends about when
women were keepers of the universe
when gardens proliferated
between our thighs and even if
we were hacked and scattered
over the earth   temples
would grow from the bits of us
even the cosmos   seriously
the cosmos stemmed from us
in other words we were
the beginning the origin of the world

say all this has vanished
like the great auks
those awkward flightless birds
mistaken for witches
say those legends have gone
into a kind of extinction
and we have grown silent
as an underground stream
and every now and again
one of us would amass enough
steam to plunge off a cliff
like a waterfall shouting a name
and even though the noise she made
was thunderous nobody heard
and she disappeared and we did not ask
where she went to or why
heart   atom   danger
wants not to break apart

and it is hard to say
why our ears and tongues
went off to be pilgrims
in the valley of silence
without leaving a note
or how the thorns got
plucked from our throats
but now they've returned
we must make up the beds
and unpack the cases
we must listen to every
unbearable thing until we too
can name our unbearable
things until the sound of
unbearable is deafening

and it is like the fairy tale
after a long spell of sleep

it is wake up people it is
time to find our way back
bridges are burning
and towers have collapsed
and some will say the witches
are returning but really it is the
world asking to be made again
so let us bring flowers let us
bow down let us worship
and reveal our scars let us

ADVICE FOR PLINY THE ELDER, BIG DADDY
OF MANSPLAINERS

Great Man, now that you are dead, allow me to squeeze your hand. The sage
bushes in Umbria are heavy with bees, so I'm killing them with hypnosis. I
am a mere woman—inferior lettuce—but I understand swoon aka *mirabilia*.
I fill this cup with nectar and offer it to soothe your Vesuvian wounds. I share
your love of baths and classification and sure, if we have to point to a god in the
sky, why not call him Thunderbolt? I too believe sewers are *the* great architectural
invention. I do all my searching on roads. It has been two thousand years, so we
can forgive some of your assertions. The sea mouse who helps whales find their
way by parting the brows above their eyes. The one-eyed humans and sciapods
with umbrella feet, the whole exotic bestiary. If I had no mouth but could live
off the smell of apples I'd move to Kashmir—scratch that, maybe Sussex.
Once a month, when the blood comes, I go out to lie in whatever field I
find to feel the scorch rise and the crops wither. Our powers are much
depleted. I can stand among men in full swing of my *menstruus* and
nothing will dim their ability to tell me about me. There are birds
I can't name at the window this morning and dogs in the valley
beyond, who are using their bell-shaped lungs to announce
their happiness again and again and again. Nothing has
changed. We worry about the wane and winnow. In
your time perhaps the ladies used bits of cut-up
smocks but these days we have menstrual cups.
Desire is still a kind of ruin—that silly bird
fluttering against the window net,
trying to get in, the body's steady
lilt toward oblivion. They say you
had a sister, like Shakespeare's—
mostly overlooked. That it was she
who first noticed the smoky clouds
that sent you on your way. Dear
Pliny, I guess you never heard the
one about curiosity. The cat is real.
The earth never tires of giving
birth. If you get too close
to a volcano, you should
know it may erupt.

Roots

after Frida Kahlo

It is a common dream
of the childless to lie
down in the mystic womb
of the earth and give birth
to vine or bird, something
to root us to the living.
I too want to believe
in *the vegetable miracle*
of my body's landscape,
to reassure the chick
who fell from the chimney
last night, It's okay,
this cardboard box
will not be your eternity,
these soaked oats you accept
into the querulous ravine
of your throat might help
you live.
       The point of hunger
is to remind you to live.
I too wish for a window
instead of a torso, if only
to see how ravenous land
can be—flotillas of igneous
rock spread out like a farm
of intestines, a prehistoric
sea of rotting teeth. Of course
the body of earth is the body of us.
Does it matter which myths
you believe in? There is always
a love-struck woman sleeping
on her back in the cold

while her raging lover hurls
stones.
        And don't volcanoes
make the same jet engine kettle
shriek dead lovers make centuries
later, saying, Why didn't you wait
for me? So why cultivate vegetables
when you can plant your own body
in the desert, when you can be
your own moveable oasis?
                  Shush.
Lie back. Regard the vast caverns,
the mouths. Remember how it was
to feed at the breast, that wild
need to hold on because you knew,
even then, that the mystery
of beginnings was held
in explosions.
               That the end
may be a whimper but beginning
is always rupture *or is it rapture,*
and if I were ever to be
worshipped as bearer
of greens, goddess of grain,
I'd say, Place a pillow under
my head, bring me fruit
instead of a candle.
Drum up a feast of rain.

In a Dream I Give Birth to a Sumo Wrestler

I'm on an island, which could be Gulliver's Brobdingnag.
An elephant bird is handing out tote bags. The evening is warm
and the creature in my arms is perfect with his thong and sleek
man bun, his real smooth buns. *Did it hurt?* Amrita Sher-Gil leans in
to ask. She appears as she is in *Self-Portrait as Tahitian*. I stare at her.
She's beautiful, but also, she's at eye level. *The birth?*
I say, *Of course it hurt, look at the size of him.*
I was told a story once of a mother in Rome, who when her child
threw a statue across a room, said, *My son, my strong son!*
That's the tone I use now about my boy. Just look,
it's time to feed him again, to bring him a bowl of fatty meat
and cabbage. I want to kiss him but he's quick on his feet,
lifting his pillowy legs in the air. We watch him, Amrita and I,
smacking the insides of his thighs. I long to impress
her so I compare his unrestrained flair to Balzac
emerging from the catacombs, eating a sack of pears.
It's here I understand I'm in the bloom of a dream,
that all this stems from the image of my brother in an adult nappy,
looking confused at the mess coming out of his body
like one of my distempered puppies. My mother, my father,
and I scrub shit off the floor for hours. We take turns. Go up
and down stairs with bucket and mop, pass him and give
his forehead a stroke. He's powdered and wan on the stripped
mattress. *Okay?* we ask. *Feeling better?* And I tell you,
sometimes the charge of this body gets too much,
like love, it grabs hold of your ankles, an understory
of weeds, when what you need is to swim out.
Would you paint us, Amrita? I ask, back in the dream.
*Like one of those woodblocks from the Edo period, in a teahouse
by the river, or as travelers passing a shrine in the mist.*
She understands I mean all of us. Mother, father, brother,
my sumo boy. She exits the dream with a wave, saying, *Sure,
leave an envelope under your pillow, and tell the world
I'm not the Indian fucking Frida Kahlo.* The next morning
at breakfast, we are a family of wrestlers, hungry for the feast,

ready to charge into one another. We say nothing of our aching bodies,
our soiled feet. Nothing of how my brother has gone from room
to room at night, switching on lights to make sure we're alive.
I still feel the birth wounds, how lonely it was after he left.
It's so quick. The topple, the capitulation. How easy to forget
that all we have are these bodies. That all of this—all of this—is holy.

Instructions on Surviving Genocide

In the study of comparative
trauma, it is important to ask
how much have you suffered,
and is it enough? *Hello, are you still
breathing?* No, this is not the time
to speak of boots and grenades.
Just nod if you want to be counted.

> Courtroom exhibit one: Make way
> for the man with the funny mustache.
> Gosh, there are so many of them.
> Our enemies slip infertility pills into
> samosas so we must be vigilant.
> Your family was wiped out? Come.
> There's a seat for you on the truck.

Remember, cities rise and fall
just as names of streets change
from uppity colonial settler to local
yogalord. In any event, refuse to be
devoured. Do not mess with the birth-
places of gods, most massacres being
propagated by god-whisperers.

> Meanwhile, a woman in the square
> shouts about how there are many ways
> of taking a stand. The way she chooses
> is naked, with one leg here, the other there.
> Are you scared? They'll stuff her mouth
> and make her watch, subdue her
> ethnically recalcitrant womb,

and despite all footage, the event
will be blurred from the nation's memory
span. Do not believe those who say it was
wonderful before the war. Listen instead
to those saying, *Get out, get out while you can.*
They work the streets, exhuming bodies,
finding safety pins instead of buttons.

There was a grand theater here,
a library, houses with balconies. This was
a good place with good people. Fathers were
weavers of rugs. They passed down secrets
through needles as if they already knew a day
would come when all the able-bodied men
would be taken away. The women . . .

What more can be said about women?
Leave it. If history were a picture show
and we kept editing the bits we didn't like
snip   snip   snip
all we could agree on would be a field
in the sun. A field is just a field after all.
Until you're introduced to the worms.

Until you find the bottles of rum,
the coats glazed with pox. All handed
out freely. Take one, take three! The victory
of genocide relies on an understanding
of pathogens. To receive a harpoon
you must be able to spell *extirpation*
followed by *this execrable race.*

There comes a point in the battle
when the last international watchdog
is forced to leave the country. Reader,
I know you're prone to anxiety. This
is when it happens. The lagoon, the ambush.
Bullets raining down in a no-fire zone.
Quick, into my echo chamber.

There were people who roamed
the kingdom of earth without need
of signposts or flags, while others
made a business out of hanging
over cliffs, trapping the breeze in jars.
But tell me, how will you breathe if your
country that was your sky, ancestor, song,

is now the size of a parking lot?
We're getting to the point, it's almost
always about land. The flap in the door
that promises *garden garden* is really a trap.
This morning on the radio, they were
remembering S, but it could have been R
or A, any litany of the alphabet.

They began with sad music to cue
the genocide. Bagpipes, perhaps,
or violins? But it could have been a lyre,
sarod, suona, djembe—some ensemble
of wind, string, horn, or better still,
they could have gone straight
to the throat of a well—

dirge, wail, ululate. We can agree
we need trigger music before talking
of tragedy. I don't trust orphanages
filled with adults or neighbors who
keep track of your auras. Look, when
you're unloaded from the truck they'll point
to a road. You'll see a meadow, a river.

A house in the distance. Inside,
perhaps a feast of chicken and rice.
The soldier in the beret will say, *Go there
to your people, your native people.* I won't
lie. It shimmers. Everything beloved. A vision,
a roof, waiting and complete. Take this picture.
The sweetness. Then walk the other way.

The Comeback of Speedos

I'll keep this brief. I remember the shock of Mr. G's tiger-striped trunks
at the Madras Gymkhana Club. Nothing to conceal, everything to
declare, like a Mills & Boon hero. Shiver of ball and sack, acres
of hairy scrub. We could not imagine such freedom for
ourselves. To slice through chlorinated depths
with a little basket of dim sum on display.
We were girls. To open our legs
was treason. We held
our breath.

FACE EXERCISES FOR MARIONETTE LINES

One's prime is the moment one was born for.
MURIEL SPARK, *THE PRIME OF MISS JEAN BRODIE*

My face, you understand the task at hand.
To make your way among cabbage whites
and meadow browns without grimacing.
To thrash stalks of ragwort and other less
esteemed wildflowers until their heads
spiral off like planets, clearing a path
from glade through wood, so you can drive
the earthforce into your marionette lines,
which is to say—prevail. Appearances must always
appear to be effortless. Think of how the young
speak of desire. How they understand nothing
of the years of their prime, clinging to tiny
churches of bereft, tiny churches of peg-like legs.
Wittering away their treasures without realizing
how many times the earth will turn over
in tide and eclipse. How one day in a car
speeding through a foreign land, someone
on the radio will announce they've discovered
water on Mars, and it will make you gauge
things differently. For instance, how clever
it is to keep country roads narrow because it makes
the landscape seem large. And it will not occur
to you how many seasons you've lived through,
or where exactly you left your prime—maybe
in a bar in Zanzibar—only that you are separated
from it and left with this face in the rearview mirror.
And because you know the story of Sisyphus,
you practice your Marilyn Monroe kisses—
pucker and blow, pucker and blow,
hoping to seduce the great oaks

while activating depleted areas of collagen.
Do not ponder the drought-worn fields.
Can't you see? From here the wheat
is still golden. It gleams.

I Found a Village and in It Were All Our Missing Women

i.m. Margaret Mascarenhas

I found a village and in it were all our missing
women, holding guns to the heads of birds.

They'd heard the voting had begun, that it had been
going on for years without them.

They knew their sisters had been bribed with gas
cylinders and bicycles, that even grandmas

grabbed bags of rice in exchange for the ballot.
They showed no resentment.

Left all their gold to the descendants
of a Mongolian war princess with whom they shared

a minor percent of DNA. I found a village, a republic,
the size of a small island country with a history

of autogenic massacre. In it were all our missing women.
They'd been sending proof of their existence—

copies of birth and not-quite-dead certificates
to offices of the registrar.

What they received in response was a rake
and a cobweb in a box.

The rake was used to comb the sugarcane fields
for wombs lost in accidental hysterectomies.

The cobweb box became an installation
to represent the curious feeling

of sitting backward on a train—of life
pulling away from you even as you longed to surge ahead.

They were not fatalistic. Could say *apocalyptic fatigue*
and *extinction crisis* in quick succession

after several rounds of mai tais.
I found a village with a sacred tree

shot free of all its refugees,
in whose branches our missing women had hung

colored passport photos of themselves.
Now listen:

A woman is not a bird or chick or anything with wings,
but a woman knows the sound of wind

and how it moves its massive thighs against your skin.
The sound of house swallowed by sinkhole,

crater, tunnel, quicksand, quake.
The collective whoosh of a disappearing,

the way a gun might miss its target,
the way 21 million might just vanish.

CONTAGION

When it is forbidden to touch, I will lean out of the window
and throw you a pillow. Light during plague-time can be so sullen.
Look at the girl who walks the deserted streets, chewing on stalks
of cabbage. She has been sent to find charlock. Returning, she may fall
off a bridge or be bitten by a dog. She knows it's important to have fun
while you can. There's always a nun who mixes ash with food
to destroy the taste of anything good. Even soldiers who heave
their flea-ridden boots across carpets of hyacinth understand,
mountains can be barriers for only so long.
Let's return to the open window—the girl below.
Doesn't she believe she's modern, that whatever this ague is,
it can't touch her? There are red crosses on doors, altars
on thoroughfares. The physician wears a wax cloth
over his mouth. Here begins   *wait*   can we say it?
Pestis. Shhhh. Shut the door. Everyone alive, get on your knees
and pray. Can you hear? There's a sound of shoes clattering
above. The girl and her sister are dancing. They hold
each other's waist and lean into the corrupt air,
which is like the pillow I threw you—soft receptacle of love.
They don't hear our appeals for care, *Girls, remember to wash
your hands.* Nor that other voice, *Traitors, what have you done?*
They dance. They keep dancing.

Tree of Life

Bengal men self-quarantine on tree to keep others safe
HINDUSTAN TIMES, MARCH 30, 2020

It could be romantic to sleep in a tree
with all the sounds of the forest around—
insect cacophony, elephants in musth.
I have always loved the word *rut*. A seasonal
glut. The opposite of looking through
a window to a never-ending view
of wives washing dishes in the sink—
Simone de Beauvoir's idea of the domestic
abyss. But reader, she had silk curtains
and chandeliers. She had multiple lovers
and appointments with Sartre in the Jardin
du Luxembourg. It is dangerous to romanticize
anyone's life, especially low to purge the nobility
of the poor, so let me not say how much I cried
watching Satyajit Ray's *Pather Panchali*,
especially the part with the kids running
through fields of kash to watch the train
of modernity pass. More poignant if you know
the director's wife had to pawn her jewels
for the film to be made. The goodness
of some women—they almost levitate,
like the girl in the film, child of the forest,
how she picks thorns from her feet like stones
from rice. And the crone, how I love the crone.
How all this sadness builds like a raga to bring
on rain, which the girl rushes into of course—
ripple of water lilies, siege of cranes. How all
this joy leads to death. There are no spare rooms
is the point. In the film or real life.
There are no spare rooms, so these men
who've returned from the city are put in a tree
to quarantine, a tree that strangles its hosts

as it walks. Munificent, shade-giving banyan
that hurls down roots as trunks, in whose leaves
God Krishna is domiciled. Krishna—who talks good game
about the temporality of the body, while enjoying
the bliss of so many pretty bodies—understood
the material world as one huge inverted banyan.
But as we're here in this reflection, why not
enjoy the fruits, why not leap from branch
to branch like a hoopoe? Which these men do,
I suppose. Their good wives leave supplies
at the base—rice and oil, cooking implements.
It goes like this for days, this story of seven men
in a tree, surviving a twenty-first-century pandemic.
Men who say they're pleased not to pass on
any bad city virus. And because the news is so full
of horrors and counterfeits, can't we for once
just succumb to the romance before us?
Forget that the tree is moving,
that one day its phantom limbs will tap
against our door. Till then can't we stand
by our windows and stare at all the desolation
and sweetness? Can't we adore the convoluted
roots of our attachments? How they complete
us. My god, how this living is a hymn.

Homage to the Square

I still like to believe that the square is a human invention.
And that tickles me. So when I have a preference for it then
I can only say excuse me.
Josef Albers

You loved the squareness of square,
the hardness of it, its resistance
to symbolism.

But a thousand squares
is a kind of tenderness,
don't you think?

Square is earth,
is ground, is pura, is prithvi,
is everything we stand on,

is no ambiguity,
is perimeter, is geometry,
is where I place my feet, my head.

You loved colors because they lie,
because they make you see what you want to see.
You say firm and wild,

and I see a saffron cube,
which is actually my father.
You say warmth and softness,

and I see clouds, or are they wildebeest?
Charging into forests with muscles
I thought were extinct. Sartorius, gracilis.

Electrical storms. No. Wings. No.
The unbearable suppleness of door hinges.
All descriptions are pedestrian.

You stand at the boundary, holding a sign:
This way to Squaredom. And it is nothing
we understand square to be today—

limited, hemmed in, conservative.
Instead—draw up, draw up from these squares
the heavy containment of earth.

It has been sitting there so long, waiting
for your toes to make contact. The reliability
of mud. It flows upward, through bodies,

through heads, into sky, which is not a square,
darling, but the roof that has always been above
and around us, a generous goblet of blue.

I Don't Want to Be Remembered for
My Last Instagram Post

→

If our ancestors really
lived in dust we could
kneel and emancipate
them from roots
of tamarisk

and they'd tell us it's better
to live as nomads. Not to get
too attached to the land or
ourselves, not to jump from
a window at our own party.

Even the calmest of us
will one day follow a thread
of gold and find a way to hang
from it, instead of riding its feathery
back into town. It is better

to begin as a bricklayer or cutter
of stone before becoming
a poet because so much depends
on who settles where and
who tramples whom.

History is a ruin from which
we emerge—whose temple,
whose hill, whose house we
are now happily sitting in.
How else to explain

the country's new name,
the tanks on the horizon?
Strangers ask to be let in to
reclaim their old treasures but
are confused by the redecoration.

There were times we used
to haul out our mad in circuses
for Sunday tourists so we
could measure the distance
between them and us.

Now we trawl through airless
square boxes with calipers,
leaving messages on virtual shrines,
counting out followers. Beware
the Pied Piper who promises

a holy land. A man in Jaffa
told me how he collects fragments
of bulldozed houses—somebody's
hearth, somebody's pewter knocker,
somebody's father walking

down a corridor in a dark suit
and oversized glasses. One day
he will make a whole thing
from these shards but until then
we feast in a graveyard.

I'm trying to tell you something,
but the helpline only works
during business hours. We
need new scribes for this ravage.
Here is my distress signal:

but perhaps I'm standing
too far to the left or right
because I can't find a filter to describe
how talking about you is really
talking about me.

a knee and holding candlelight
vigils, what are we really saying
and is it enough? Imagine the world
as an aquarium. How some
are always staring from behind

Despite what they say,
there are still delicate cloisters
of coral to get lost in. But
as you descend you begin to see
creatures unchanged by time,

there are pinwheels ablaze
and glowing tentacles that
reach to embrace you. Language
falls away and everything is
either light-giving or light-filled

I arrive at meetings
with an olive branch and a gun.
I too want to lift everyone
by the wrists and insist on how
mysterious all this is, how precious,

Even if we use hashtags and refuse
to cry for stones that have been
destroyed. Even if we believe we are
making a revolution from
the platforms of our boxes by taking

the hard polished glass,
while others cling to crags,
surviving on breadcrumbs.
Of course, there are beautiful
colors and bright schools of fish.

blind giants with trapdoor
mouths and leggy behemoths
patrolling the sponge gardens.
It becomes difficult to breathe
and it is cold, but see—

filigree, rib, fringe—unfurling
like flowers. The question
is how long can you go with
your prayers and what pictures
will you take while you're there?

Everyone Has a Wilting Point

You know things are dire
when temples get down
on their stony knees to pray,
when leaders stand in dehydrated
wells to fold hands and stare
at the sky expecting it to tear open,
when women wait with empty
pots in streets for the water tanker
god to arrive. It is hard for a temple
to crouch. Harder still for leaders
to look sincere, especially when
they are men with melancholy
upper bodies that do not inspire
ideas of fertility. The reservoirs
are empty and the rivers are full
of shit and it would be easy to say
that the leaders too are empty
and full of shit, but let us assume
that they are as beautiful as temples
in their centuries of genuflection.
Let us assume their joints
are arthritic from all the groveling
and they know what it means to fall
into the crack of earth and feel
its parched tongue slither across
their backs. Perhaps it reminds them
of their own tongues—how they went
from tongue-lickers to the tongue-licked.
Surely one of them will understand
how the history of political slobbering
is in fact a lesson in condensation,
how maybe what we need instead
is a mountain and two lovers
who have been set apart
so they can send messages

to each other through a cloud,
because if we are going to pray
to fill the furrows, why not
also pray for love, why not seal
the pockmarked ground by resting
against our wilting points and point
to sky and point to plow and recite
the hundred names of desire, so when
the rains decide to fall they will bring
a plenitude enough to quench this drought.

TIGRESS HUGS MANCHURIAN FIR

This
far north
the sun rises
and sinks in the
same spot. Insects
announce the apocalypse
and fog moves through all
the uncountable hours like a
bright gray scar. The forest is
awash in a dial of light more
luminiferous than a Canaletto. I
misuse the words *forest, woodland,*
jungle because I have never walked
alone through forest, woodland, jungle.
I say Canaletto because I long to be in a
place of light different from this place of light.
The days are bleak and I've forgotten how to dress.
I don't believe you need to wear a loincloth to prove
your sincerity, or know how to sew your own lederhosen.
I begin my diaries with *Chipko means to hug in Hindi.*
And even though I know the history of the ecofeminist
embrace is fierce, not cute, it helps me understand the gap
between my life and the denuded hillside. There are remote
places in the world—Garhwal, Siberia—where trees are extracted
like teeth to make way for the king's summer palace, for a sporting
goods company. With this new virus, hugging has been outlawed, so the
picture of you, dear tigress, has sustained me more than a triple-glazed room
in Yakutsk. If I had been sent to collect spring water and found myself in a desert,
I too would want to lie down in a pile of broken glass just to feel a piece
of my lung. We are asked to leave things to chance, but if the future
is really a slaughterhouse, then why not stake our territory?
Imagine saying to the tree: *I'm cold and alone*
and I need this small fire to burn.
Imagine the tree replying:
Come seedling, let's dance.

Poems Lull Us into Safety

Each day arrives with new misgivings.
We say *dodged a bullet* when we mean
   love has been killing me steadily
   since I was sixteen. We say *manic*
   when we mean *I can no longer sleep*
   so have forgotten how to be myself.
   The dog understands these things
even though she has not read Foucault.
   She is not schooled in deception,
is oblivious to the problem of defective
vaccines in China and how the female
dragonfly feigns sudden death to avoid
male advances. She wouldn't get the irony
of a cop in Uttar Pradesh scaring a criminal
   by making gun noises with his mouth
      because his gun is jammed.
Not *bang bang bang* but *thain thain thain*
      because Hindi, not English.
      She doesn't believe in language,
         only in dodging cannon fire.
      She sits on the path to the beach,
      her whole body a temple to epizoa.
      She has been twice abandoned,
is overly attached to the needles of casuarina,
   will not let me stroke her unless I recite
   a poem. It has to be a singular thing
      that lulls her—liturgy, utterance,
   the way breath tethers us from birth,
         is taken away or restored.
         The dog is an epistemologist
even though she cannot spell the word.
      She knows what she knows.

After a Shooting in a Maternity Clinic in Kabul

No one forgets there's a war going on,
but there are moments you could be forgiven
for believing the city is still an orchard,
a place where you could make a thing grow.
There is always a pile of rubble from which
some desperate person struggles to rise,
while another person wraps a shawl
around their shoulders and roasts
marshmallows over a fire.
This is not that.
This is not bomb dropping from sky,
human shield, hostages in a stream, child
picking up toy that explodes in her hands—
although there's always that—hope is a booby trap.
This is the house you were brought to after crossing
a river, leaving the mountains and burnt fields
behind. A place of safety where you
could be alone with your own
startling power.
Not *Why were you out? And why
wasn't your face covered? And who told you
to climb into that rickshaw?* But *Here, prepare
for this most ordinary thing, a birth.* And this is not
to ask what it means never to see someone again,
but to ask what it means not to make it past
the first checkpoint of your mother's gates.
Never mind all the wild places
outside—
the mud-brick villages, the valleys and harvests
and glasses of green tea. Or even to say *I am here
to claim the child of Suraya,* because you know
this to be impossible. Even if you could bring a man
to recover your sister's corpse and the newborn,
where do you go from here? You still have

to consider the bodies, the bullet-ridden
walls, still have to find the small
window of this house and take
in the panorama.
See—it is raining outside and men weep
for their wives, and perhaps the entire world
is an orchard that has detonated its crimson fruits,
its pomegranates and poppies and tart mulberries
to wash these floors red, and those of us who stand
outside this house know that nothing will flourish
here again. Like crowds who gather
for an execution, we can only ask,
what does it mean to be born
in a graveyard, to enter
the world, saying,
Oh thief, oh life.

They Killed Cows. I Killed Them.

In the future we might all be vegetarian,
and this life will seem barbaric the way
a corset was or eugenics. We might look
at this man being secretly recorded, bragging,
They killed cows, I killed them, and wonder,
where was his mother? She might have spoken
of his childhood, how it was poor but decent,
how like that blue god's mother she too gaped
into her son's wide gob and saw the universe
once. Or she might have told the story of how
he was led astray by a band of men in uniforms.
Not brownshirts but pleated brownshorts
in which they practiced ideological calisthenics.
How she's been standing at the crater's edge
saying, *Here, kitty kitty kitty,* ever since.

Because this man, her son in the undershirt,
dear cadre, cow vigilante, he's no gladiolus.
He sighs. Even his mustache is pusillanimous.
Maybe he was a Romeo in school. Maybe
he wields this stick to reclaim what he misses
most about his body, or maybe it's always been
his dream to squeeze the messy limbs of this country
into a svelte operatic shriek. The camera gives us
a glimpse of his chin dumpling. He will go to jail
a thousand times without passing go, without
stopping to plant a tree or collect clean underwear.
He admits it was wrong to allow his boys to record
the killing. *Jai Shri Ram.* Silly to leave evidence
behind, even though they always go free,
even though the young lads enjoy it so.

And Qasim? The man they killed,
the green meadow of his life come to this,
didn't his mother also once confuse the dirt
in his mouth for a galaxy? Didn't he believe

a dying man had the right to ask for water?
In the future when people complain about how Gandhi
should have made a comeback, when comparisons
are drawn between YouTube and the *Upanishads*,
will they notice the bystanders in the frame,
their shabby shoes shuffling like lapwings
around the bloody censored blur of Qasim's body?
Will they speak of the difficulty of watching him
thrash around for an invisible rope to steady
him home, the difficulty of us watching them
watching him being killed?

Or is that an illusion too? The way a magician
might swirl his cape to reveal his assistant
is really a robot. *No damage done here folks!*
The way we enter the rooms of our past
like gunshots to say, *Surprise, I'm still here.*
No point carrying blossoms in your pocket
instead of a meat sandwich. Because even if
you do not walk the earth exultantly, even if
you avoid disposable plates and mourn
every glacier and string a lattice of pearls
to the giant monument of love, there might still
come a day when you are hauling refrigerators
on a truck, or taking the children to a fair,
and when death arrives you must let him
strap you to a telephone pole, you must look
into his ten-headed face, and say, *Flay, brother, flay.*

CELL

Even if you could walk through the corridors
of your body, you would not know which rooms
to enter, which were full of stone. Inside you
there is so much water. A mountain range
in the north to stave off invaders, a desert
in the bacterial colonies of the south. Here
are city buildings, yellowed, without windows,
busy with the making of vaccines and handbags.
Here a double helix strung up the length
of your spine like a flurry of Tibetan prayer flags.
Between these outposts the messengers dart,
carrying tubes of animal hide, pigeons on their backs.
Some ride rams, some travel with consort shadows
in chariots across the skies without once stopping
to look at stars. When they arrive it is almost always
the same. They must remove their sandals and wait
by the mouth of the cave—its fold of skin,
a curtain to trap the wind. They want to tell
you the great fires are still burning, the bees
won't give up their unions, the harvest is both
moon and autumn. You are not alone.

SELF

And when they ask what kind of animal
would you be, I always say gazelle or lark,
never cockroach, even though they'll outlast
us all. Once I dreamed I had a body with two
heads like those ancient figures from the Zarqa
River—bitumen eyes, trunks of reed and hydrated
lime, built thick and flat without genitals, nothing
shameful to eject except tears. We all want to be
monuments but can't help shoving our fingers
in dirt. Imagine a life in childhood—one face
to the womb, another to the future. What we remember
is the road, peering through a lattice at dusk,
the trauma of burial. Will we have terra-cotta
armies to take us through, will we be alone
with the maggots? How good the rain is
after a failed romance. Never mind the muddy
bloomers. We are appalled by life and still,
any chance we get we emerge from the earth
like cicadas to sing and fuck for a moment
of triumph. The shock we carry is that the world
doesn't need us. Even so, we go collecting parts—
an afternoon by the sea, a game of hopping on
and off scales, nose low to the ground, looking
for that other glove to complete us.
Here I am, globe, spinning planet.
Tell me, Why are you not astonished?

COLLECTIVE

While you're away the rules will change. Overnight the town
becomes a fortress, your marriage a morgue. Spies are installed
in adobe walls and a new tax is levied on sleep. Your daughters
are taken from their beds and you stand for hours to offer bills
of surrender. Down the hall a mason builds a chamber to incubate
memories. The treasury starts trading currency for cigarettes
and a lightbulb keeps track of infidelities. Your body—
that mountain you carry around—begins to develop craters.
One day your heart will collapse, this economy too, but for now
a man in a pink ball gown is restoring lost matchsticks to their boxes.
When the final bell rings and the curtains part, we climb a ladder
together. Some stand above to measure the wind. Makers of bread
take subsidiary rungs. No doubt we'll change positions. A king
may drink from a beggar's well, the sweeper's wife will emerge
from the leeward side in a three-piece suit and tie. Try not to search
for meaning. If you need proof you're alive, regard the oar
in your hand. Look at all this glass, the vaulted ceiling.
Someone is hammering a skylight into the roof.

NATION

Sorry, the coastline is closed today, but we can accommodate
you offshore. Our stevedores will help carry your belongings.
This way please for a complimentary spray of DDT. No jewels
allowed in quarantine, leave them with me, but when you're free,
we'll give you a house with a chain-link fence, an orange grove
and an AK-47. Forget where you came from, forget history.
It never happened, okay? We need soldiers on the front line.
Of course we can coexist. We say potato, they say potato.
We give them their own ghetto. Listen, sometimes you need
to dance with whoever is on the dance floor, which means,
sometimes you need to drive large numbers of their people
in a truck across the dark. A few may die, but then ask,
If I'm not for me, who is? It's absolutely forbidden to touch
the women's knickers. If things go awry (shit happens),
better to dump their bodies in the desert. No drowning allowed
on international TV. No talking about jasmine-scented streets
either. Understand, friend, the conscience is a delicate broth.
Sometimes it feels good to be bad. Step over this field of bones.
Here's where the wall is going to go. If you're not happy,
you can leave, but tell the world we're building a new country.
Entry is free and we welcome all!

SPECIES

When it is time, we will herd into the bunker of the earth
to join the lost animals—pig-footed bandicoot, giant sea
snail, woolly mammoth. No sound of chain saws, only
the soft *swish swish* of dead forests, pressing our heads
to the lake's floor, a blanket of leaves to make fossils
of our femurs and last suppers. In a million years
they will find and restore us to jungles of kapok.
Their children will rally to stare at ancestors.
Neanderthals in caves with paintings of the gnu
period. Papa *Homo erectus* forever squatting over
the thrill of fire. Their bastard offspring with prairie-size
mandibles, stuttering over the beginnings of speech. And finally,
us—diminutive species of *Homo,* not so wise, with our weak necks
and robo lovers, our cobalt-speckled lungs. Will it be for them
as it was for us, impossible to imagine oceans where there are now
mountains? Will they recognize their own story in the feather-tailed
dinosaur, stepping out of a wave of extinction to tread over blooms
of algae, never once thinking about asteroids or microbial stew?
If we could communicate, would we admit that intergalactic
colonization was never a sound plan? We should have learned
from the grass, humble in its abundance, offering food and shelter
wherever it spread. Instead, we stamped our feet like gods,
marveling at the life we made, imagining all of it to be ours.

COSMOS

Each night I take my boat out to you, asleep under
the oaks. I thought I saw a lotus creep out of your navel,
which means you got my cable. Remember when we were
young and the end was a black hole at the edge of forever,
a million light-years away? Now we're in the thick of it.
See how it swallows everything—a jungle leopard feasting
through our bloodline of mongrels. Have you noticed,
lying there as you do in moonlight, how a hurricane viewed
from outer space looks like a wisp of cotton candy?
Or how the seagull nebula resembles a section of rosy
duodenum? Down in the market a man speaks of finding
anger in his left armpit. Another talks of space debris
drifting into the River Lethe. No one can tell me
why we paint demons on our houses, except that it has
to do with entries and exits. The monsters are never
far away. I want to believe the earth is a single breathing
organism. I want to keep going with this bronze body
of mine, turning and turning the gears. You left no note,
so I must assume you woke in the middle of a dream
and took shelter in the forest. Maybe you're already
in the beauty of that other world, growing planetary rings
and gardens of foxglove. You know this skin is a thin
partition, citrus and bergamot sealed in. It's always
ourselves we're most afraid of. Take this vellum
and pin it to your bodice. Let it say *We were here.*

THE CORONAPOCALYPSE WILL BE TELEVISED

Those aren't birds you
hear, just their corresponding holes in the sky.
ANSELM BERRIGAN

Silence is never magical in this republic.
We believe in procession, in utterance,
in honoring the dead, not by shutting up
for a minute, but by going into the street
and beating a drum. This is how we greet grief.

With rose petal and drink and dancing limb.
We are not the type to sew our lips in protest,
nor will we go mad if you string us upside down
and expose us to the shrieks of dying rabbits.
Our gods are in favor of cymbals.

It's the other thing that kills us—the field
of uninterrupted grass, the on and on of nothing.
How can you bear it? There have always been
two kinds of people: those whose hearts
can stand to live beside volcanoes,

and those who write letters to the neighbors,
asking when's a good time to beat the carpets,
and is it possible to tone it down on the piano?
This funeral song is different. It asks for us
to die alone, to step into a well with inflamed lungs,

only to find we're not in water, but drowning
on dry land. So sure, we can bang our pots and pans
from balconies, we can write notes of gratitude
and send them out in air balloons so those alive
on other planets can witness our disintegration

as though we were actors in a silent film,
our movements wild and jerky. Do they see how
sad we are, how aghast. Do they laugh

at the irony of our government's title cards:
"Breathe Easy!" & "Don't Worry!"

"Nothing's Going to Tank the Economy!"
Who'd have thought the end would be so complete?
We keel over and get up again, the mud
on our knees too hungry to scream, an invisible
orchestra of violins directing us from the wings.

Variations on Hippo

i.m. Margaret Mascarenhas

I

Every summer I vow to find
a way back into my body.
Usually after a friend dies,
or is about to die. How to explain
the perpetual weirdness of stalking
yourself? It's like taking a boat
out to sea only to look back
at the land you've just left
behind. Of course the cliffs.
Of course shanks, stretch marks,
volcanic body ablaze with all
its filigree of cacti and hurt.
It's a kind of recognition,
the way language unfastens
to reveal meaning. Of course
the hippopotamus is a horse
of the river. Which came first,
horse or hippo? Does it matter?
We drink wine and dodge meduse
in the water and when the boat shirks
home it's hard to believe we're alive
to the world and all its monsters.
There is my body—in search
of the perfect summer hat,
patient as a mantis flexing in the sun.
She pretends not to hear when I say,
Here is your chariot, embark,
please, take me back.

II

M—we were driving past
the Hippodrome de la Côte d'Azur
when I heard of your death
and began writing this poem,
which confused you momentarily
with another friend who died
in summer, also too young,
also a poet. We drove through
a storm so ancient, drops the size
of cowrie shells smashing against
the windows. In Mesopotamia,
land between two rivers,
where they domesticated the horse
and invented writing and chariots
and beer, they had so many words
for what I'm feeling but none
I can pronounce. *I don't want to die,*
is what another friend writes,
and this is what I say aloud.
I don't want to die unless
it's like looking up through
a circle of gum trees so tall
your neck pinches just a little
to take in the sweep of them.
And maybe leaving could be
just that. Breath tunneling
out of us into a column of blue,
the waxy sheen of branches.
But leaving's complicated,
and when you consider
the word *dies* has been hiding
in our bodies all along—
small treacherous rose.
Remember you and me
in your car in Goa, stuck

for hours in traffic, cursing
the shabby tourists, the road
widening and shadowing into dark,
so much of it ahead of us.

III

For years I've been carrying
a memory in the seahorse
of my head. That little campus
of hippo that said the reason
I'm afraid of closed spaces
is because once when I
was tiny and living in the house
I still dream of, I got locked
behind the bathroom door.
For hours, or was it minutes,
I stood, listening to my mother
on the other side, coaxing me
to turn the key this way and that,
when all I wanted was to float
through wood, to come alive
the way my toys did at night,
drifting down from their shelves
to play. How even now in public
stalls or grand Tuscan bathrooms,
I will not bother with dodgy locks—
simply hover and hope no one storms
through. And even though I've since
been told it wasn't me stuck behind
that childhood door, but my brother,
who could not express in words
what must have been a trauma,
some kind of transference,
it does not alter my fear of being
hemmed in. Think of the smallness
of coffin, the largeness of death.

Somewhere, it is still summer
and I am a child stuck behind
a door, and have lost no one
except nearly—the boy Mark,
who almost drowned in the rock
pools at a picnic lunch. But there
is nothing false about the way dread
moves through my briny, mouse-like
body, which holds the knowledge
of these future losses, sharp as electrical
shocks that endanger from foot to spine.
Listen, all we can do is wait. Mother,
dryad, someone, slide me an opening.

A Dress Is Like a Field

A dress is like a field. Lift a hem and flowers
will fall. Fold it in a wooden chest and weeds
will lay their fingers against its cotton heart.
A dress is sin. Take Marilyn. Take subway grate.
Take *You must have had to paint that on you.*
Flamenco ruffle, zipper, Cleopatra in gold lamé.
Little. Black. Something. When we were girls,
we played at dressing up—Mum's swimsuit
with the built-in bosoms, a lesson in seduction.
The past is a yard in Wales. My mother
and her sister in matching seersucker frocks,
hands in pockets, high collars, the wind
making petticoats of their hair. They join
a ship of sisters. Mothers with needles
and thread, holding bolts of cloth against
their chests, thinking, this will do, this will sail
them across the years. A Singer sewing machine
in Madras. My sister and I in handmade smocks
with floral bibs and frills. Aspiring zazous with high
socks and lacunas of knees. If I had daughters
I'd dress them in velvet suits with cummerbunds
so they could roll down meadows and scorch
the wilds of their insides against grass.
A dress needs only a mosquito net to be a bride,
and later, as it yellows in a bag, it will dream
of being a factory girl, a schoolchild, something lumpen
and uniform, to recognize itself in the other.
A dress never loses its sense of the dramatic.
It knows how to languish across a washing line,
how to beckon from a mannequin, how to sit
puddled on a floor. See this riverbank—
there's a row of them, unbelted, unbuttoned.
The river calls for an afternoon of love,
a picnic, clots of copper maple. Legs of bone,
seams turned toward the sun. Nothing

like abandoned shoes, which glow with horror,
the piles at Dachau, trains, gunshots, dead bodies in water.
A dress is a forest of memory. Its damask skin,
its armpits of toil and wonder. Even the holes
are altars to fairy tales, reminding you how once
you were so small. Once your waist was a secret nation.

POSTCARD TO MY MOTHER-IN-LAW WHO AT SIXTEEN IS CHASING BRIGITTE BARDOT IN SAINT-TROPEZ

At sixteen we are a rare species. Rocks share our secrets. The gap between who we are and who we want to be is epic. Those who love us would secure us with safety nets. We long to fall. Try not to fall. Dopamine is rapacious—a long glittering beach that runs through us. Dear Editta, nothing can shake you. Already you are the most chic person in your family. When you go home, you will sew a pink-and-white gingham dress just like Bardot's. Your friend in the hotel—the other Italian girl— her name is gone. But for now, you are both unmoored in the streets of Saint-Tropez. There's Jacques Charrier! He's buying cigarettes. He's so close, OMG . . . is that a pimple, how does he get to be with *HER?* Sixty-one years pass. Marriages are wrecked. Brigitte's. Yours. The dangers you chose litter the coastline like dregs. Only a picture remains of you in that dress, face turned toward the sky as though it were the past, which is no place to come back from. So much wet sand. And the story of course. Your father in his faltering French, asking for the good road, *La vie est bonne;* the stranger answering, *Yes, life is good!*

TOGETHER

You can be born by a river but will die at the foot
of a mountain. Your left hand murders a chicken,
your right prays for its safe passage. Duality shows you
the gaps. When I think of *together,* I don't think
of Advaita or Hegel, but of music in a room,
everyone tapping their feet to the same tune.
My mother in a dance hall in Wales, mouthing *love me do*
with the Beatles before they went big. How I can see her through
a froth of beehives and charmeuse even though I don't know her yet.
How there are times when your body and you are friends, not this mad
chasing each other along the shore, and the people you've lost show up
complaining about passports and broken necks. You can sit for hours,
and it's like sitting in a language together. There's no point asking them
to wait or come back because these moments are already vanishing
like the countryside. It doesn't mean you won't ever go out foraging alone
or mistakenly rush past yourself in a slur of department store windows,
but living is a thing we do together. The neighbor who loans
you a tranquilizer, the person on the ladder above
who throws you a hydrangea. Bands split up
when what you want is for them to stay bound.
Just as love will always insist it's the first time,
everything that passed before was just bad
juju or a rebound. I want the world in my bed, for us
to tumble forward as though we'd each given birth. Not heir,
not orchard, just a thing in our arms that depends on us,
so we can shout above the wind, *Be bop doo wop.*
For the sound that returns to take us
to the brink of nuclear harmony.

MANY GOOD AND WONDERFUL THINGS

What more am I to say? Our kind-hearted Sirkar has done everything
possible for us to protect us from the cold. We are each provided with
two pairs of strong, expensive boots. We have whale oil to rub in our
feet, and for food we are provided with live Spanish sheep. In short, the
Sirkar has accumulated many good and wonderful things for our use.
KALA KHAN TO ILTAF HUSSAIN, DECEMBER 27, 1917

History too has a hard time remembering
the black waters they crossed, the small
mountain villages emptied of men.
Death was different then. History is always
reinventing itself. Say what you will,
but clouds have remained more or less
the same, and leaving home is still leaving
home, whether it's on a jet plane or climbing
the steep path behind the house with a roll
of bedding on your back. But to die in a faraway
place whose name you can't pronounce,
for a king who isn't really yours, is a sadness
history still hasn't figured out. History
has been pushing for republics since Lucius
Junius Brutus, but men are hardy, is the point,
or bullheaded. And you'd think the glories
of lice making mansions in their shirts
was a paradise they could do without,
that trench-living would make them walk
across the front with arms held high, saying,
Take me quick, I wish only to enter the realms
of God. History tries not to be sentimental,
although letters give things away. One fool
longed for a flute—the world is burning,
but he wants to play. Others were gluttons,
mercenaries, spies. The wise asked for opium,
But write *sweets* or *dainties,* they said,
otherwise the package might not reach.

History needs to forget the dead who cover
the earth like heaps of stones, who write:
Mother—is my parrot still alive?
Mother—do not go wandering madly.

Sometimes it feels as though the rain
has been falling all your life and the girl
you married will tire of tending the cattle.
Do not worry. This is war, where the women,
like metaphors, are always steadfast and beautiful.
In history's version she sits under the peepal tree
with your Victoria Cross pinned to her sari.
She has been waiting since 1918 and she is waiting
still. So let us speak of love the way we always have,
by asking, Have you eaten, darling? And what price
did you get for the goats? And, Of course,
I miss you, but the earth is hard and the sky,
distant, and if I had wings I'd fly to you.
In Marseille they said we looked like kings.
History cannot really say what happens to men
at war. So listen: At night I feed on stars.
Do not ask about the cold. They have given
me whale oil for my feet and someone
told me if I carried a piece of raw onion
into battle, the bullets would not find me.

I CARRY MY UTERUS IN A SMALL SUITCASE

I carry my uterus in a small suitcase
for the day I need to leave it
at the railway station.
Till then I hold on
to my hysteria
and take my
nettle tea
with
gin.

BACTERIUM

All my cousins are self-made.
Small beings with no stomach for defeat,
able to create, maintain, and destroy themselves
like a divine Hindu triumvirate. Have you heard
the one about the god who stubs his toe on a wall
of the universe, making a hole for the Milky Way
to flow through. Milky Way that is really a river.
River that is really a goddess. Goddess that is really
a mother who drowns her seven children to lift a curse.
O Ganga, you see where this could go. Things begin
pure but quickly get sullied. Downstream from the pharma
companies, residents of housing colonies grow obese
on effluents. A rogue tribe blooming in the camps of the north
have abandoned their tuning forks. Me? I believe the gods send us letters
in envelopes we can't open, and this makes up the atmosphere.
Most of what we understand about the past is written
on the skins of dead animals, and still, we know
so little. Perhaps we shouldn't get too close.
Everything's a war for space in this kingdom.
Grab your SOS gear. Survival depends
on the blink of penicillin. Brethren,
here are the steps to the Murky Way.
The temperature is fine. Don't be afraid.
Glide down to the river, drink.

A Possible Explanation as to Why We Mutilate Women & Trees, Which Tries to End on a Note of Hope

Begin with trees. Consider they have yearnings too.
Bereft trees and sinister trees and trees that send
letters of distress to the prime minister.

I come from a country that understood these things.
Whole treatises devoted to describing which trees
long to hear thunder before they burst forth buds,

and which trees need the touch of a young woman's foot
or the sprinkle of wine from her mouth before deigning
to bloom. Whole treatises on the desires of pregnant women

and how they had to be tended to, otherwise the birth
would come to grief. On the subject of blooming
we can't be outdone. So husband, go, go find me

that out-of-season mango, bring me a golden stag
that can preach the law, fetch me sand from the bottom
of the sea. (Forgive this heavily heteronormative fantasy.)

Remember these cravings are two-hearted, vicarious.
A swan on a throne under a fringed marquee?
I'll take that too. No request can be too outlandish.

Think about a country whose creation hymn
isn't *In the beginning was the word* but *In the beginning
was desire.* How affirmative. A place that has earth

and sky for parents. (Motherfucker, are you listening?)
Gaze up at those pillars adorning temples and stupas
and notice how there are always ladies, foliage, hips,

ferns, shalabhanjika, because every auspicious thing
has to be fertile. And think of the mastery of making
God's home the temple's womb chamber.

Return to mother, return to death. (Freud came later.)
Think of how a person might feel displaced by the powers
he will never have, how this may lead to stories

about mothers with malignant breasts, or a group
of demonesses who move together like the Pleiades.
How it could be said that they invite the knife,

the way ten million trees invite a massacre.
Call it highway, call it development, but listen,
and you will hear the bubbles in their trunks,

the cavitations. And everywhere you turn,
this poem will lead you back into a cave,
into underground chamber, into capitulate.

Oh rage, still yourself, submit to the mystery
that gave you breath. Know that to harvest
your own longings you have to put your nose

to the ground. Here is the garden, here the mud,
here are the tides that propel the sea. Put your mouth
to that flower, that wound. The rest is magic.

What Mr. Frog Running Away from Marilyn Monroe Taught Me about #MeToo

In the powder room beside the stairs
I keep a portrait of Marilyn.
Not a Warhol original but
one of those cheap museum prints
I bought instead of a magnet.

The tree frog who lives in that room
sits on the picture frame and grins,
groin chakra exploding. Sometimes he
shifts to the book on the windowsill
so he can give her come hither looks.

At night when the many insects
and rodents come out to play
Mr. Frog uses his skills in camouflage
to blend into the blue shadow
of Marilyn's eyes. It's a kind of love

mirage with sneaky undertones
of lust because I've heard him emit
mating calls—jackhammerish—
when he should be out there
looking for a pond to cast his frothy net.

Instead, he's jerking off to cosmic dust
and when other frogs try to enter the chamber
Mr. Frog squirts them with projectile
pee. He's possessive of his queen.
The house understands—

she's his Norma Jean. But of late
Mr. Frog has displayed
erratic behavior. I found him
by the door making a run for it
and yesterday he got as far as the stairs.

He was carrying an edition
of the morning papers,
his skin a bit droopy and sad,
as if all his desires had been purged
from him by an evil (female) mortician.

On the veranda consulting
with his more colorful cousin—
the Malabar gliding frog—
he confessed to a kind of confusion
about these uneven power equations

but insisted on the purity
of his love—how he had never heard
her say no, how all of this was so long ago,
how career breaking, how humiliating.
I'm a good man, really, I am.

And even as Mr. Frog escaped
into the wilderness, cries of Me Too
came from the bushes. Ms. Bee-eater,
Ms. Kingfisher, no one had been spared.
Even as we understood the magnitude

of these allegations, the wind blew
as decision makers do, knocking down
a few trees to appease the crowd—
and, afterward, restored his green kingdom
as if nothing had ever happened.

TIGER WOMAN

after a nineteenth-century Mughal painting of two men
in pursuit of a tiger woman

No one writes poems for the handsome sidekick
who barely makes the frame—there to collect his master's
clothes by the river. He has seen those creamy, solid thighs
a thousand times, knows what lies behind the shrubs
of pink—body bags, flies. You would rather hear
about the woman, the chimera beneath. You want to know
what the air was like that febrile day, how the sun crafted
a way to shine upon her fan of hair. I understand. You would
rather talk about the things only you can see—
the tiger paws, the tail, a body transformed underwater.
But if you listen to the sidekick, he can tell you why all the old cities
made fortresses of themselves, how those soft, green mounds
evocative of breasts should have been painted as ruined blocks
of apartments instead. You do not get to have an empire
without squashing someone else. Lean in and he will tell you how
the summer hunts are so frequent, even the heap of muslin
on the bank is overcome with sweat. Even the cicadas
who are sawing the afternoon in half seem to be signaling a threat.
On this occasion, the tiger woman escapes, but the sidekick
knows, eventually the body fails. How many times
has he found himself dreaming of bird feet and a plumed tail?
Some way to take flight. You see, the river is sweet
and brims with carp, but the water's edge is
skin, stained with curses and blood sacrifices.
In one part of the world something is always blooming.
No amount of washing takes the smell off him.

We Will Not Kill You. We'll Just Shoot You in the Vagina.

It's true. We're useless without our vaginas.
How will you rape us? How will we birth daughters
and sons? I understand. We should laugh.
It would be better if we did, Mr. Duterte.
In India, our leaders say eating chow mein
excites the hormones, which provokes rape.

And if you can't prevent it, may as well enjoy it (rape).
In one of your 120 languages, the word for vagina
is *bisong,* which sounds like a headlong bird, not chow
mein, which good mothers don't feed their daughters
for fear of provoking, you know . . . Mr. Duterte,
may I call you Rodrigo? We should laugh.

O'Keeffe did when they said she painted vulvas (laughed).
Her flowers didn't wear jeans or stay out late. Rape
doesn't happen to respected ladies. Dirty Duterte,
#BabaeAko, what do you have against vaginas?
What about Sara and Veronica, your daughters
& their drama queen vaginas? What about chow mein?

Personally, I'm against MSG, FGM & chow mein.
In Hindi, one of India's 780 languages (I laugh,
not to be competitive, but we'd win), the word for daughter
is *beti,* do you know how many lost daughters—raped,
unborn, disappeared? One longs for a Venus flytrap vagina
or *yoni,* the most delectable word for cunt. Duterte

Harry, P-Rod, PDiggy, Digong, Rody (Duterte)—
is Viagra Your Excellency's version of chow mein?
Who dares call you impotent? You who want vaginas
shot at, you who smooch factory workers, you who laugh
and say as long as there are beautiful girls there will be rape.
There's always a beautiful beti (daughter).

Our leaders warn us to keep our daughters
at home like cars, so they won't get scratched, Mr. Duterte.
They tell us to call our rapists *brother* while they rape
us and afterward everyone can go out for chow mein
because nobody agrees to do it on the first try (laugh).
Mr. President, we have teeth in our rebel vaginas,

and they don't need chow mein. Our vaginas
have learned to shoot. They laugh and talk back (rapacious
beasts). Our daughters feed them poems, Mr. Duterte!

Microeconomics

i

A woman begins with peas. She adopts one, then a second. Pretty soon she's got the rest of the pod sheltering under her cot. The peas keep her company like djinns in the garden. When the other women come over, they roll them around in their thin fingers, saying, This one would make a good match for my turnip, don't you think?

ii

Hearing this, our woman immediately thinks of death. How when someone is gone, the first thing you ask is: Was it old age or the dreaded C? Was it fatigue, a dodgy heart, the loan shark? Not: I'm sorry, or do you think us getting together to watch plays all night is symbolic of our collective need for immortality? But how did that poor sod die, and how close is death to me?

iii

Losing her peas was akin to losing her identity, which is the only thing she really had, according to the bank that loaned her the cash. It was control and freedom and her way of rejecting the patriarchy, so like some medieval anorexic nun she starved herself for the greater glory of her peas.

iv

Trying to rise from poverty to the middle class means being asked on a daily basis whether you prefer things subsidized or free, which is a trick question that fails to account for the history of oppression. Our woman wants to say, Don't talk to me about ordinal utility. My first house was a sari wrapped around bamboo poles. My second is made of brick. Let's keep the progression going.

v

Our woman wants to keep her investments together. She could make a blanket of peas to store in her cedar chest or save them for a winter soup, but winter sometimes goes on too long, and her husband's will is strong. He has already caught her licking the floor, gathering cobwebs in her maw. Every day he goes into a crushing machine at work and grinds himself into silica dust.

vi

When it rains, as it often does, our woman takes her brood to the neighbor's hut, which has a tin roof instead of straw. The weatherman prophesies a decade of floods. Nobody wants to lose what they have. We are family until we are not.

vii

Is it meaningful to ask whether to save the house or the peas? Or is it more meaningful to place ourselves on weighing scales and say, Here is my life, this is its price.

viii

There's been a spate of suicides. Our woman decides to return one pea to the bank. Hearing the soft *thup* of its skin as it falls, she admits she was hoping for a fuller sound. Don't worry, she says to the terrified legume, you have not been forsaken, and throws after it a clump of fertilizer and the poems of Hafez.

Macroeconomics

One man sits on another if he can.
One man's heart beats stronger. One man goes
into the mines for another man to sparkle.
One man dies so the family living at the top of the hill
can eat sandwiches on the lawn. One man's piggy bank
gets a bailout. One man tips over a stranger's vegetable cart.
One man stays home and plays tombola till all this blows over.
One man hits the road like a pilgrim to Shambhala, child
on shoulders. One man asks who's going to go out and buy
the milk and eggs? One man's home is across the horizon.
One man decides to walk there even though it will take days
and nights on tarmac with little food and water.
One man is stopped for loitering and made to do squats
for penance. One man reports fish are leaping
out of the sea and sucking greedily from the air.
One man eats his ration card. One man notices how starlings
have taken to the skies like a toothache,
a low continuous hunger, searing across the fields.
One man loads his gun. One man's in charge of the seesaw.
One man wants to redistribute the plums. One man knows
there's no such thing as a free lunch. One man finally sees
the crevasse. One man gives his blanket to the man
sitting in the crevasse. One man says there should be a tax
for doing such a thing and takes it back. The ditch widens.

This May Reach You Either as a Bird or Flower

for Varavara Rao

Sooner or later we must return
to the rooms from which we emerged.
The earth of your childhood is the earth
of mine, even though it may seem we live in
two different countries. You are a dangerous
poet in yours. I am trying to be one. In every
republic there will be some who walk down to
the water with life vests and bread, while others
lead soldiers to trapdoors in the cellar. You stand
at the edge, beating a drum. They say you've been
standing there sixty years, drumming, drumming.
Sir—are you warm? Are the crows bringing you the
latest terrible news? The mobs haul bodies from beyond
the campfires with leaves tacked to their eyes and throats
filled with dust. You should know there's been a breach. The
curtain is not made of iron. The offspring of your arrests have
formed their own political party in prison and are spreading
rebellious thoughts like a virus refreshed after a summer rest.
We must consolidate while there's oxygen left. A day will
come when we are gathered in a courtyard for a historic
photo, and asked to denounce the pawns, the black-and-
white squares, the horses and rooks. Everyone but
the crooks. It will no longer be possible to say
your homeland is not my homeland
because it doesn't speak English.
The languages we love will be
thrown in a ditch. A country
forgets how many countries
it's been. Nothing is gentle
about memory. The sky
speaks in howl, grass
whispers back. We
are already on
our knees.
What else
can we
do but
resist?

PETARD

After you were banished to the desert for months, you came home
to find the house occupied. A stranger had moved in and befriended
the dog. Three families of squirrels built nests in the shuttered

windows, and termites were hard at work in the bathroom, building
a cathedral of sand. The stranger was in the planter's chair reading diaries
and love letters you'd left behind. There was a vodka martini in a chalice,

wind chimes working their best John Denver rendition from the porch.
When the stranger saw you, he said, *Wife, welcome home,* and for a moment—
confusion. You were not one of those poet-saints whose homes and tombs

were as moveable as their desires. You had not offered up these rooms and said,
You have no bed, take mine. You have no family, be mine. Supper was laid out
on a yellow tablecloth and there was even a vase of bougainvillea drooping

into the soup. It had been so long since you'd seen clouds, so the stranger and you
walked out to the beach to marvel at those cumulonimbi, which in every language
are harbingers, heaped and towering like volcanoes floating low above the sea.

The stranger opened his arms as though gathering an imaginary bouquet
of flowers, as if to say, *Thanks for all this. It means a lot.* Your heart exploded
with its own goodness and exploded again when it considered all it might lose

or might already have lost. You thought about that woman in Iceland who joined
the search party to look for a missing woman, who turned out to be herself.
How it is a search every day. To wince or not to wince. How at academic

conferences on Hamlet you want to talk not about language being rhizomic
or vectorizing the text, but about an aunt who lifts one cheek casually
midconversation, to let loose wind, as though it were news rushing to be told.

Rotten Grief

This morning I misread *Tantrism* for *Tourism* and it's been downhill
ever since. Elephants are dying in the Okavango Delta and no one
knows why. A man I love crumples into himself on a railway
platform away from home. My sister calls to tell me about
her aged cat, who keeps collapsing, then rising to roam
the house in wobbly confusion. It is all falling, falling.
A poet on the internet talks about a Jewish legend,
where we are given tears in compensation for
death. I would cry about the perfectness of it
except I'm incapable. My ophthalmologist
has made a diagnosis of dry eye so I
must buy my tears in a pharmacy.
I think of what this is doing to
all the rotten grief inside me—
unable to create salt bathing
pools to fire up my wounds,
this body powered by
breath, dragging its
legs through
the vast
summers
that have
lost their will to
transform me. All
the unknowing we
must accept and fold
like silk pocket-hankies
pressed against our chests.
The theory of spanda in
Tantra advises you to *live*
within the heart. I'm a tourist
here, so bear with me, but imagine
a universe vibrated into being. All things
made and unmade by a host of small movements,

my favorite being matsyodari—throb of fish when
out of water. Just the word *throb*, you understand, hints
at longing, but also distress, and suddenly, language opens.
All the etymologies I used to think were useless in the arena
of bereavement are echoing over the great plains of beige carpet,
saying, *We interrupt your weeping to tell you the world is real, rejoice!*

The elephants in the Okavango are keeling over like ships. No one
can say why. A die-off sounds worryingly like a bake-off but
without the final prize. At night I squeeze drops into my
eyes, whispering the magic words, *Replenish, ducts,*
replenish. If you play elephants the voices of their
dead, they'll go mad for days, searching for
their beloveds. To fall is never an action
in slow motion. The snap of elastic
in your pants, *going going gone.*
Belief caving in like a bridge.
My heart, your heart, the
elephants'—here's a
crazy thought—
what if they're
dying of
grief?

OCTOBER FUGUE

The year is laying down its leaves
like an oil spill along the coast of Kamchatka.
A sweep of toxic yellow, dead seals, starfish—
a whole darkening orchard. Persimmon, quince.
This morning I fell over while trying to straighten
the curtains. Perhaps I saw reflections of trees
in the windows and got confused, the way birds
often do. Perhaps I wanted to understand
what it means to slam into buildings of glass
and fall from the sky in large numbers.
This is the roof of the world. Out there,
flares of a burning taiga. Didn't they promise
respite from the air strikes? Who promised
a life, golden? Take this pillow from under
my head. We're running out of provisions.
How far can we flee with headscarves
and slippers? In all this mist it's easy to forget
how a season of dying can still be flamboyant.
We risk breaking our necks but we should
make a go of it. Shouldn't it be now?

Do Not Go Out in the Storm

Say the words *Bay of Bengal*
and *Buchenwald* one after
the other, and they sound
beautiful, just as *landfall*
does. And then imagine it:

> the first sign
> of a tree
> or beach
> after so many
> days at sea.

> > We are always in the midst
> > of life even if we think
> > we're just skirting the rim.
> > Say *landfall* again, and it
> > means something else—

the eye of a cyclone hurtling
toward the coast like a planet
out of control. Sometimes we
track the danger for days and
there's time for evacuations.

> Sometimes we
> embark on
> trains not
> knowing where
> they go.

> > Often, we are given warnings.
> > Do not go out in the storm.
> > A postcard followed by silence.
> > Hurry, the lorries are coming.
> > You better run into the woods.

But who wants to leave
behind the warmth of a straw
bed, to abandon the flowerpots
and pets? How to haul the family
trunk to higher ground?

                        The
                        days
                  of waiting
                        are
                  a lull,

                              the slow continuous rocking
                              of a boat. When disaster comes
                              there's no time for prayers.
                              The radio announces:

            We regret to say, this will unfold with force.

In the records of shipwrecks,
my favorite causes remain:
insanity; presence of captains'
wives, and other women;
boys larking with gunpowder.

                  Irrawaddy,
                  Kutupalong,
                  Belsen. How many
                  bodies committed
                  to the deep?

                        After the flattening, there are
                        miracles. Babies alive in the debris,
                        an entire novel smuggled upstream
                        in a tube of toothpaste. A honey
                        collector's perfect machete.

What matters is that we believe
in our own goodness. Later,
those of us who survived
will drag our boots through
ruins and mud embankments,

        draw maps
        of where
        the displaced
        were
        flung,

                cease to be bystanders. We choose
                sides in history, take note of all
                the broken jetties and roofs of
                asbestos, all the splinters of church
                spires tangled in electrified wire.

Some of us will sit in the dictator's
bathtub and wash ourselves. Some
of us return to the apartment
alone and find only outlines
of paintings on the walls.

        A seven-year-old
        boy turns
        his head away
        from a pile of
        emaciated bodies.

                After the cyclone, I walk home,
                a wreckage of trees at my feet.
                This is how the world outlives us,
                making itself anew—the dark leaves
                beneath, so soft, so forgiving.

Listening to Abida Parveen on Loop, I Understand Why I Miss Home and Why It Must Be So

This frugal diet of living
is getting to me

Sometimes in the desert
the wind will blow through my shell-shaped ears
and whisper a sea song just to taunt me

If the endgame is to renounce house
mother father husband sibling succulent child
to go in search of better hummus and woolen blankets
to choose one dog and run for the border
I'm not sure this contest was made for me

What if the dog ignores me

What if he refuses water from the tin cup
I lay out for him   what if we become estranged
like Enkidu   ancient wanderer   and his herd
What if my dog finds himself a family
of wolves and abandons me

What if I felt my heart was taken out of me

I could begin each day with praise
could serve and work without once uttering
the word *home*   could write on multiple
clay tablets   could even practice hieroglyphs
the symbol for voyage
a torn-out eye
falling man with blood streaming from head
Apis   Nandi   cosmic bull running into me

I would do it if it meant I could go back
and everything would be as I left it
bread on table   bowl of salt
apple tree   river and its stepping-stones
returned to me

What if it was better to live with radiation
than with war   what if home was Chernobyl
what if the well was poisoned but the birdsong
made up for it   what if the ghosts
of all the shot dogs went to live underground
with the worms   what if you didn't wake up
asking did it all really happen to me

What if we were birds forced to spend
our lives in air   to mate and sleep
on the wing   to rope round and round
the earth in circles and have screaming parties
what if we were never meant to settle
would you still search out my beak midair
would you still find me

We are homesick everywhere
even when we're home   we are empty things
that need filling
we are always lost in love   never found
please come find me

What if this minaret was like the last
tooth in my head   unsteady
and enflamed with devotion   what if I'm finally old
and ready for the plant of rejuvenation
but no one's offering it to me

We're at that moment in the journey
when we've hit a wall and the only way to scale
it is to use your voice with its inflections
and ditches   its rough grain and longing
What if god on the other side of the wall
was equally alone and in need of company
What if we replaced *god* with *home*
What if I was ready to become nothing
What if I understood there was no me

Would you carry me to this divinity

End-of-Year Epiphany at the Holiday Inn

Softly, first, over egg bhurji and juice—
This country is losing her soul,
a man in a wheelchair is beaten
for not standing for the national anthem.
Breakfast was once a noble affair,
not this litany of selfies. I know it's ridiculous
to think countries have souls, that this one
could be feminine. I know I should have faith
in happiness and child wonders
who will rid the earth of plastic. Oh yes,
I know the probability of a person coming
to their knees at an airport, crying, *Who am I?*
is high, and most people will walk by
because time is always calling. We must believe
everything will be all right because people
are still having babies and taking them to the sea.
So what if a man is slaughtered and set alight
for love, for a slab of dead cow, for reasons
sacred? So what if the waters are rising,
and those seas will soon be upon us?
We must live in the moments we're given.

Louder now, in the lobby of the Holiday Inn—
This country is losing her soul,
because politicians declare our daughters
safe as long as they're parked at home,
and geniuses proclaim the national bird
so holy it impregnates with tears.
I know I should be kinder on feedback forms.
I know you don't want to tell me how
to live unless you're selling me something.
No one's really listening unless you're on TV.
But there are people who still grow heirloom rice,
who long for roses to assault the walls
of their homes because they believe in beauty

and her graces. And perhaps part of surviving
is to keep your knees soft, to bear grief
that the missing will always remain missing.
So when the new year arrives with the golden
light of a late Sunday morning, whispering how
everyone you love will be kept safe, you take
those promises deep into the pink
          of your mouth, and you swallow.

IT HAS TAKEN MANY YEARS TO SEE MY BODY

Thus far the work looks somewhat bland and uninteresting. Then come the final steps, the first being khulai, *literally, "opening up." Every outline turns crisp, every detail comes to life. The work begins to open its eyes, as it were.*
B.N. GOSWAMY, *THE SPIRIT OF INDIAN PAINTING*

i. *Muladhara*

If we could reconstruct the temple of our bodies,
we all know what we'd change first.
A little demolition work in the zone of belly,
some gutting around hips and bum,
a coat of paint after weather-stripping the face.
I would kneel first at the hillocks
of my breasts and pay obeisance.
Praise the dainty bud of squirrel's tail
that made them. In the miniature painting
of me, the background tree meant to symbolize
my beauty would not be laden with pomegranates.
Kumquats perhaps, or plums.

ii. *Svadisthana*

The first room they gave me was a prison cell
with a tattered divan and a dog named Akhmatova.
I entered it a mole, proprietorial, in love with solitude.
Then they moved me to a castle. Then a mud hut
without a full-length mirror. At night I walk
the passages with head bowed and covered
like those Rajput women in the miniatures,
striding out in rain to meet their lovers.
Back in the room, I step out of my carapace.
Strip off the lobster tail and corset.
Blood pumps and I stuff my knickers
with what I find. Moss and hemp, delirium,
accordions of linen. I bump into Louise Bourgeois,
carrying a basket of marble eggs. She looks at my breasts

and says, *You do not get anywhere by being literal,*
except to be puny, then hurries off to set up
The Return of the Repressed.

iii. *Manipura*

It would be a lie to say I didn't dream of largesse.

iv. *Anahata*

As a girl I enjoyed synchronized swimming
like Alexander McQueen, even though I often forgot
the routines, and one of the other girls said, *You're so lucky*
you're flat, meaning the opposite. Neither she nor I knew
about the devastating chic of Jane Birkin's tiny pets.
We had not seen Donald Sutherland hover over
Julie Christie for four long minutes in *Don't Look Now,*
two naked golden planks. We did not even know
about the seashell-breasted women of certain Indian
miniatures, small-statured saplings, squatting
to squeeze water from their hair to feed a thirsty crane,
blouse hitched up the bee-stung slopes while feeding
antelope. We had been prepared only for the giant
heaving smother of Ajanta's apsaras or Silk Smitha,
for decades of backaches. *Thanks,* I said. *Yeah, thanks.*

v. *Vishuddha*

So
when I find
the lump all these
years later, my first thought
is that I should have been
spared this ignominy.
After all the hum of
pancake itty-bitty,
a stone in this,
really?

vi. *Ajna*

In the room
I've been given now
the walls are made of glass.
Outside is the desert and a city.
Beyond that the sea. A construction site
below has been abandoned. So many meticulous
rectangles arranged like open graves waiting to be filled.

vii. *Sahasrara*

One day at sunrise you come across your body
and greet it, as though it were a guest or traveler.
You bathe its legs and sprinkle it with sandalwood
and rose water. You may even have to protect
your eyes with oversized sunglasses, like those pilgrims
who can't withstand directly the gaze of the deity.
You will enter the inner chamber, this final doorway
in the infinity of doorways, and there will be no mediator.
No one to collect money or say a prayer, just a tapestry
of virgin wool, hanging on a washing line with wooden
pegs. You walk toward it in devotion,
touch it in all its fraying places,
bring it to your chest,
starving and full.

Hope Is the Thing

And sore must be the storm—
That could abash the little Bird
Emily Dickinson

These days I pay attention to birds.
Bulbul gorging in the yellow trumpet bush,
reminding me to drink my daily fill.
Ring-necked parakeet, flying past
my office window like a gouache
on loose-leaf paper. If we knew our death days
as we do our birth days, would we celebrate
them with garlands of wildflowers, or rush
past them in the corridor of each rolling year
with a shiver? Would we go on periodic diets
of martinis and wafers, trying to unhinge
ourselves? I like to think of hope
as an organism inside us, a cluster
of molecules into which energy flows, in
and out. A hatchery whose inhabitants
sometimes grow thin or corpulent.

As a girl I wanted a man with a healthy
jaw like Jean Gabin or Dharmendra.
I was thwarted by a teacher in Madras
who sent me home to lower the hems
of my skirts, shrieking, *Too short, too short!*
Hope died there that day and once again
in a motel overlooking a strip mall in Ohio.
It's all right to be momentarily proud
of being an unfashionable shapeless martyr.
It's okay to feel the loneliness crash into you
like a boat bashing against a pier in a hurricane.
You'll find your way back into the world
by climbing into the wet fur of dark
and measuring all the absences in the park.

You'll turn and say to whomever your companions
are, *Don't worry dears, we're not far off.*

I'd like to grow up to be a woman
with a crown of silver hair and a walled
garden, but what I have instead are a pack
of piebald dogs and some pots of mint and sage.
What is this greed of wanting more,
of baking four and twenty blackbirds in a pie
and expecting them to sing, when you know
that a twelve-year-old girl, who makes her living
picking chilies, has just died of exhaustion
walking home? And as you learn her name,
Jamalo, and are figuring out how to mourn
her, someone else will say, *Look,*
the flamingos have returned to Bombay.
Look how this carpet of pink brightens
the day. It's the difficulty of reconciliation.
This with that. Jack and his box.
The continual threat of being startled.

Maybe what you miss is what's simple,
which isn't childhood, but that bird
of prey holding the air with its claws.
If you knew it would cost nothing
to keep your wings open like an albatross,
that you could go ten thousand miles without
a single flap, that it has to be this way,
this glissando between soaring and falling,
you could pack up your indignations
and move toward the phone booth
in the sky. A god at the door sitting
on a giant buffalo offers you a sip
of wine to make the bitterness go away.
Your final phone call is to the future,
We're fine, you say. *We're all going to be just fine.*

SURVIVAL

Dear ones who are still alive, I fear we may have overthought
things. It is not always a war between celebration and lament.
Now we know death is circuitous, not just a matter of hiding
in the dark, or under a bed, not even a slingshot for our loved
ones to carry, it changes nothing. Ask me to build a wall
and I will build it straight. When the end came, were you
watching TV or picnicking in a field with friends? Was the tablecloth
white, did you stay silent or fight? I hope by now you've given up
the fur coat, the frequent-flier miles. In the hours of waiting,
I heard a legend about a woman who was carried off by winds,
a love ballet between her and the gods, which involved only minor
mutilations. How I long to be a legend. To stand at the dock
and stare at this or that creature who survived. Examine
its nest, marvel at a tusk that can rake the seafloor for food.
Hope is a noose around my neck. I have traded in my rollerblades
for a quill. Here is the boat, the journey, the camp. If we want
to arrive we must push someone off the side. It is impossible
to feel benign. How many refugees does it take to build
a mansion? I ask again, shall we wait or run?
Here is winter, the dense pack ice. Touch it. It is a reminder
of our devastation. A kind of worship, an incantation.

NOTES

Creation Abecedarian

This poem was written in response to statements made by the Indian minister in charge of higher education, Satyapal Singh of the BJP, in January 2018. He stated that Darwin's theory of evolution was wrong and demanded it be removed from school curricula because "nobody, including our ancestors, in written or oral, said they ever saw an ape turning into a human being." In 2019, during a discussion on the Protection of Human Rights (Amendment) Bill, he said: "Our culture says we are the children of rishis. I don't want to offend people who believe that we are children of monkeys, but according to our culture we are children of rishis."

The Stormtroopers of My Country

On December 11, 2019, the Citizenship Amendment Bill (CAB) was passed in the upper house of parliament in India, with the idea of providing sanctuary to people fleeing religious persecution from neighboring countries and allowing them to apply for citizenship, amending the old CAB, which prohibited undocumented migrants from becoming Indian citizens. The new law was viewed by critics of the BJP government as being anti-Muslim because the bill only offered refuge to six communities—Hindu, Sikh, Buddhist, Jain, Parsi, and Christian. Muslim religious minorities, such as the Ahmadis in Pakistan and the Rohingyas in Myanmar, would not be considered. In February 2020 anti-Citizen Amendment Act (CAA) protest riots erupted in New Delhi for four days, the most serious communal violence the country had seen in decades, with forty-two people dead, hundreds injured, houses and shops destroyed. Amnesty International accused the Delhi police of committing serious human rights violations. Amit Shah, India's Minister of Home Affairs, has called undocumented migrants from Bangladesh "termites" and said his party would throw them out if they came to power again. Internet services in Jammu and Kashmir were cut off on August 5, 2019, and there continues to be a ban on high-speed internet, making it the world's most digitally starved region with the longest-ever internet shutdown imposed in a democracy. The right-facing swastika symbol in India represents good luck and prosperity. In the early 1920s the swastika was adopted as a symbol of the German Reich. Arundhati Roy has likened India's CAA to "the 1935 Nuremberg Laws of the Third Reich."

Why the Brazilian Butt Lift Won't Save Us

This poem was written in response to a BBC news story, "Is 'Brazilian Butt Lift' Surgery a Risk Worth Taking?," November 22, 2019.

Advice for Pliny the Elder, Big Daddy of Mansplainers

This poem is a rejoinder to Pliny the Elder who in his encyclopedic *Naturalis Historia* stated his belief that menstrual blood was so dangerous that a mere drop could kill bees, cause seeds in gardens to dry up, make a man's sword useless, and destroy whole fields. Pliny the Elder had a sister who is believed to have first seen the smoke of Vesuvius erupting. He went off to investigate and/or to help friends who lived nearby. The details are unclear, but we do know he perished there.

Roots

This poem uses a line from Frida Kahlo's diary, "the vegetable miracle of my body's landscape," written in 1944.

The Comeback of Speedos

This was written in response to an article in the *Observer* on August 9, 2020, "Tight Fit: The Comeback of the Skimpy Swimming Brief." The poem was written in Italy, where the speedo never went away.

I Found a Village and in It Were All Our Missing Women

In 2019, it was estimated that 21 million Indian women were denied the right to vote because their names were not registered on voting lists. In a separate news article, it was noted that in the Beed district of Maharashtra, more than 4,600 women who were sugarcane cutters had undergone hysterectomies so as not to miss a day of work.

Contagion

This poem takes inspiration from a story about two sisters, Maria and Cammilla, who danced their way through the plague in Florence in the spring of 1629.

Tree of Life

On March 24, 2020, the prime minister of India gave its 1.3 billion citizens four hours before imposing a countrywide lockdown. Millions of migrant workers, finding themselves unemployed overnight, set out from cities to walk home to their villages. With all public transport services suspended, they walked hundreds of kilometers with their belongings, infants, children, and even their pets. Many hundreds died of starvation, suicide, exhaustion, or in road or rail accidents. A story of seven Bengali men who quarantined in a tree outside their village in order to keep their families safe was one of the few less dire stories.

Everyone Has a Wilting Point

In June 2019, the reservoirs in the South Indian city of Chennai had run almost completely dry and the city was facing severe drought conditions. Leaders of the state performed ceremonies in temples and mosques across the state praying for rain, while opposition party members staged empty pot demonstrations demanding that the situation be met with reason rather than ritual. A wilting point is defined as the minimum amount of water in the soil that a plant requires not to wilt.

Tigress Hugs Manchurian Fir

This poem is in response to Sergey Gorshkov's remarkable photograph of an Amur tigress hugging an ancient Manchurian fir. He left a hidden camera in a Russian forest for eleven months before capturing this image, which won him Wildlife Photographer of the Year in 2020.

After a Shooting in a Maternity Clinic in Kabul

On May 12, 2020, three armed gunmen attacked the Dasht-e-Barchi maternity ward in Kabul, shooting mothers, nurses, and newborns. This poem is in response to Mujib Mashal's article in the *New York Times*, "Born into Carnage, 18 Afghan Babies Face an Uncertain Fate."

They Killed Cows. I Killed Them.

In August 2018, an undercover NDTV team recorded a member of RSS (Rashtriya Swayamsevak Sangh—a right-wing Hindu nationalist paramilitary organization), Rakesh Sisodia, out on bail, bragging about his involvement in killing a meat-trader, Qasim Qureshi, and badly injuring a sixty-five-year-old farmer, Samiuddin. Sisodia talked about how Qasim asked for water, while they were attacking him, and he said, "He has no right to drink water, he slaughtered a cow, we will kill them and go to jail a thousand times." He went on to say, "They killed cows. I killed them." In a separate incident of cow vigilantism, a twenty-four-year-old Muslim man, Tabrez Ansari, was tied to a pole and assaulted by a mob of Hindu men, forcing him to repeat *"Jai Shri Ram"* (victory to Lord Ram), which Mr. Ansari did, although the mob continued to beat him. Four days later, Mr. Ansari died from his injuries in police custody without his family being allowed to see him. According to Human Rights Watch, fourty-four people were killed in India by radical cow-protection groups from 2017 to 2019. Many of these incidents have been recorded on mobile phones and circulated widely.

Many Good and Wonderful Things

Over a million and a half Indian soldiers served in the Great War. This poem was written to mark the centenary year of the Armistice and draws from some of the letters written by Indian soldiers during the war, collected in David Omissi's *Indian Voices of the Great War* (Macmillan, 1999). "Black waters" is a reference to the kala pani, the ocean voyage believed to cause a loss of caste and social status for those who left India.

We Will Not Kill You. We'll Just Shoot You in the Vagina.

In February 2018, the Filipino president, Rodrigo Duterte, ordered soldiers to shoot female communist rebels in the vagina. He said, "We will not kill you. We'll just shoot you in the vagina," going on to say that without their vaginas, women would be "useless." The #BabaeAko movement in the Philippines grew out of anger with the misogyny of President Duterte. Duterte has two daughters—Veronica and Sara. To Sara's claims of being raped, Duterte said she can't be raped because she carries a gun, and described her as a "drama queen." Separately, in India, panchayat leader Jitender Chhatar, in Haryana, blamed the consumption of chow mein and fast food for hormonal imbalances and increasing incidences of rape.

This May Reach You Either as a Bird or Flower

This poem was written for the eighty-one-year-old Indian political poet and activist Varavara Rao who has been imprisoned since 2018 under the controversial Unlawful Activities (Prevention) Act (UAPA), which empowers the state to search and arrest without a warrant any people suspected of supporting terrorist acts or unlawful activities. Mr. Rao's family petitioned for his release after he fell critically ill in prison during the COVID-19 pandemic. Bail was denied five times. In November 2020, the Bombay High Court allowed shifting the poet to a local hospital for medical examinations. The title of my poem is a line from Varavara Rao's poem "Unburdening Song," translated from the Telugu by D. Venkat Rao.

Rotten Grief

Between May and June 2020, over 300 elephant carcasses were seen in Botswana's Okavango Delta. Elephants were seen walking in circles, appearing dizzy, and then dropping dead. Various theories were put forward about why this could be so. In September 2020, officials confirmed that the cause of death was ingesting cyanobacteria—a toxic bacteria that can occur naturally in standing water. Scientists said that climate change may be making these "toxic blooms" more likely as they favor warm water. The poet on the internet to whom I refer to in the poem is Alice Oswald—and the reference to the Jewish legend is from her Oxford Professor of Poetry lecture "Interview with Water."

Do Not Go Out in the Storm

The causes of shipwrecks in the poem are from an article in the *London Review of Books*, "Hogged," by E.S. Turner, January 22, 1998.

Hope Is the Thing

Twelve-year-old Jamalo Madkam worked in a chili field in Peruru village in the Indian state of Telangana. She was one of the millions of migrant workers walking home after India went into a nationwide lockdown due to COVID-19. Jamalo died of exhaustion on April 18 after she had been walking for three days. She was just an hour from her home in Chhattisgarh.

About the Author

Tishani Doshi is an award-winning writer and dancer of Welsh-Gujarati descent. Born in Madras, India, in 1975, she received a master's in writing from Johns Hopkins University and worked in London in advertising before returning to India in 2001, where a chance encounter with the choreographer Chandralekha led her to an unexpected career in dance. She has published eight books of fiction and poetry, including the poetry collection *Girls Are Coming Out of the Woods,* shortlisted for the Ted Hughes Award and a Firecracker Award, and the novel *Small Days and Nights,* shortlisted for the RSL Ondaatje Prize, the Tata Book of the Year (Fiction), and the *New York Times Book Review* Editors' Choice. She has interviewed over a hundred writers about the craft of writing and has published essays in *The Hindu, Granta, The National, The New York Times, The Guardian, Literary Hub,* and *Corriere della Sera.* She is a visiting professor of creative writing at New York University Abu Dhabi and, otherwise, lives on a beach in Tamil Nadu, India.

Poetry is vital to language and living. Since 1972, Copper Canyon Press has published extraordinary poetry from around the world to engage the imaginations and intellects of readers, writers, booksellers, librarians, teachers, students, and donors.

Copper Canyon Press gratefully acknowledges the kindness, patronage, and generous support of Jean Marie Lee, whose love and passionate appreciation of poetry has provided an everlasting benefit to our publishing program.

WE ARE GRATEFUL FOR THE MAJOR SUPPORT PROVIDED BY:

THE PAUL G. ALLEN
FAMILY FOUNDATION

CULTURE

Lannan

ART WORKS. | National Endowment for the Arts arts.gov

OFFICE OF ARTS & CULTURE
SEATTLE

WASHINGTON STATE
ARTS COMMISSION

TO LEARN MORE ABOUT UNDERWRITING
COPPER CANYON PRESS TITLES,
PLEASE CALL 360-385-4925 EXT. 103

WE ARE GRATEFUL FOR THE MAJOR SUPPORT PROVIDED BY:

Anonymous

Jill Baker and Jeffrey Bishop

Anne and Geoffrey Barker

In honor of Ida Bauer, Betsy Gifford, and Beverly Sachar

Donna and Matthew Bellew

Will Blythe

John Branch

Diana Broze

John R. Cahill

Sarah Cavanaugh

The Beatrice R. and Joseph A. Coleman Foundation

The Currie Family Fund

Stephanie Ellis-Smith and Douglas Smith

Laurie and Oskar Eustis

Austin Evans

Saramel Evans

Mimi Gardner Gates

Gull Industries Inc. on behalf of William True

The Trust of Warren A. Gummow

William R. Hearst, III

Carolyn and Robert Hedin

Bruce Kahn

Phil Kovacevich and Eric Wechsler

Lakeside Industries Inc. on behalf of Jeanne Marie Lee

Maureen Lee and Mark Busto

Peter Lewis and Johnna Turiano

Ellie Mathews and Carl Youngmann as The North Press

Larry Mawby and Lois Bahle

Hank and Liesel Meijer

Jack Nicholson

Gregg Orr

Petunia Charitable Fund and adviser Elizabeth Hebert

Gay Phinny

Suzanne Rapp and Mark Hamilton

Adam and Lynn Rauch

Emily and Dan Raymond

Jill and Bill Ruckelshaus

Cynthia Sears

Kim and Jeff Seely

Joan F. Woods

Barbara and Charles Wright

Caleb Young as C. Young Creative

The dedicated interns and faithful volunteers of Copper Canyon Press

The Chinese character for poetry is made up
of two parts: "word" and "temple." It also serves
as pressmark for Copper Canyon Press.

This book is set in Minion Pro, a typeface
designed by Robert Slimbach.
Book design by Gopa&Ted2, Inc.
Printed on archival-quality paper.

CPSIA information can be obtained
at www.ICGtesting.com
Printed in the USA
LVHW041749240921
698653LV00004B/19